FLY FISHING FOR RAINBOWS

FLY FISHING FOR RAINBOWS

Strategies and Tactics for North America's Favorite Trout

Rex Gerlach

Stackpole Books

Copyright © 1988 by Rex Gerlach

Published by
STACKPOLE BOOKS
Cameron and Kelker Streets
P.O. Box 1831
Harrisburg PA 17105

Printed in the United States of America

10 9 8 7 6 5 4 3 2 1

Library of Congress Cataloging-in-Publication Data

Gerlach, Rex.
    Fly fishing for rainbows: strategies and tactics for North America's favorite trout / Rex Gerlach.
       p.   cm.
    Bibliography: p.
    Includes index.
    ISBN 0-8117-0624-9
    1. Rainbow trout fishing—North America. 2. Fly fishing—North America. I. Title.
SH687.6.G47   1988
799.1'755—dc19
                                          88-16068
                                            CIP

Dedication

This book is dedicated to three fly fishermen. They are the men who have most influenced my development as a flyfisher and my attitudes towards the sport.

M/Sgt. Thomas H. Stouffer (USAF ret.) has been my casting mentor, frequent fishing companion, and friend since the late 1940s, when he was actively engaged in Pacific Northwest region flyfishing and tournament casting circles. Before World War II, "Tommy" was accuracy casting champion in the Rocky Mountain region. He could dot "i"s with a fly rod at fifty feet. He is the sort of angling companion with whom one can share a camp and the river for a month and still appreciate at the end of the trip. I named my youngest son for him.

Fenton S. Roskelley has been the distinguished outdoor writer for the Spokane Daily Chronicle since I first met him nearly three decades ago. He was a frequent flyfishing cohort from 1958 until I moved from Spokane to southern California in 1973. We shared the thrill of innumerable rainbow trout, steelhead, and Kamloops trout expeditions throughout the western region and in Canada. Without a doubt, "Ross" is one of the country's most knowledgeable, analytical, and persistent fly fishermen.

Allan Rohrer, of Costa Mesa, California, is a world-class fly fisherman and fly caster. Perhaps his greatest contributions to the sport have been the unselfish ways he works to help others improve their flyfishing skills. As he does this in seminars and demonstrations at flyfishing clubs, he also strives to instill a deep appreciation for the aquatic environments fostering trout life. As an angler, Allan is a skilled and meticulous lake and stream tactician. He seems to possess an instinctive feel for the ever-changing rhythms of the water. It's doubtful there is a more complete fly fisherman living today. Most certainly, there is no more pleasant an angling companion.

To each of these men, I offer my profound thanks for the privilege of sharing with me portions of their flyfishing lives and personalities. It has been a rich experience.

Contents

Acknowledgments

The author extends his most sincere appreciation to Bud Lilly, Allan Rohrer, and Fenton Roskelley for their assistance in acquiring much of the special photography illustrating strategies and tactics in this book. Their contributions of time and talent are gratefully acknowledged.

Thanks and appreciation also are extended to the following individuals for their assistance in the research and photographic aspects of the book.

Carol Bystrzycki, Scientific Anglers/3M; David W. Corcoran, The River's Edge, Bozeman, Montana; Yvon Coté, Quebec Ministry of Fish & Game; John K. Durbin, Saskatchewan Fisheries Branch; Joe Fisher, J. Kennedy Fisher Company; Dave Fielder, South Dakota Division of Wildlife; Jerry Gibbs, Fishing Editor, *Outdoor Life*; Robt. F. Hartmann, Kansas Department of Wildlife & Parks; Richard Healey, Lakes Systems Division; Scott Henderson, Arkansas Game & Fish Commission, Chief, Fisheries Division; Loren G. Hill, Ph.D., University of Oklahoma; Mark Hudy, Arkansas Game & Fish Commission; Philip J. Hulbert, New York State Department of Environmental Conservation, Inland Fisheries Section; Lava Creek Lodge, California; Gregg Lilly, The River's Edge, Bozeman, Montana; John G. Lindenberg, Minnesota Division of Fisheries & Wildlife; Art Michaels, Editor, *Pennsylvania Angler*; The Montana Ambassadors; Malcolm A. Redmond, New Brunswick Fish and Wildlife Branch; Tom Keith, Nebraska Game and Parks Commission; George Nelson, Manitoba Fisheries Branch; Norval Netsch, Director, Alaska Department

of Fish & Game, Division of Sport Fish;
Tom Rosenbauer, The Orvis Company;
Charles "Red" Slater, Bozeman, Montana; Scott F. Stuewe, Illinois Department of Conservation; Charles von Geldern, Jr., California Department of Fish & Game; Kendall Warner, Maine Department of Inland Fisheries & Wildlife.

Introduction

I never met a trout I didn't like. But I think I like rainbow trout the best. That's because I've been able to count on rainbow trout and their sea-going brothers the steelheads for *consistent* flyfishing action for the better part of forty-five fishing seasons.

Admittedly, like brown trout, rainbows sometimes can be difficult to bring to the fly, but only rarely have they bruised my self-confidence. I can't say the same for brown trout. Although I do enjoy flyfishing for them, I'm not certain my ego could survive it as a steady diet.

If rainbows are easier to take on the fly, they nevertheless fight with more guile, speed, and determination than any other trout. My memories of fishing for them are punctuated by jarring strikes, broken tips and tippets, and unbelievably sustained runs. Rainbows have a wildness and abandon that have left me shaking.

One of the endearing qualities of this trout is the sheer exuberance with which it often comes to the fly, even though your presentation is imperfect. The way rainbows feed reminds me of our three sons attacking the refrigerator after a rough-and-tumble game. When feeding, rainbows are free-wheeling "athletes." They'll pounce on artificial flies bearing little resemblance to any aquatic or terrestrial insect. They'll even hit non-flies such as yarn strike indicators in preference to the nymph at the end of the leader.

Flyfishing for rainbows (and steelheads) may well be the most athletic form of freshwater sport, leaving little time for philosophical reflection. You're

These recollections of rainbow trout are punctuated with memories of jarring strikes and unbelievably sustained runs.

too busy replenishing lost flies, tying fresh leaders, and staying abreast of lake and stream conditions to enjoy the contemplative side of fly fishing. A couple of my friends hike five miles each morning to stay in shape for the strenuous wading sometimes required when stream fishing for rainbows. That affords them some time for contemplation.

Rainbows are highly adaptable fish.

One of the endearing qualities of the rainbow trout is the sheer exuberance with which it often comes to the fly.

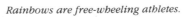

Rainbows are free-wheeling athletes.

This great willingness of both young and fully grown rainbows to abandon their natural caution occurs frequently enough to provide fly fishing high adventure.

They exhibit significant differences in behavior throughout their wide North American range, and different tactics are required to catch them *consistently*.

The following chapters describe the shifting environmental and human rhythms that influence rainbow trout fishing. We will begin by getting to know these fish and look at the characteristics that distinguish them from other trouts. Then we'll discuss how to locate ideal rainbow lakes and streams and how to find the fish living in them. These are the four Ps to consider: *prime* waters, *prime* lake and stream locations, *prime* seasons for fly fishing, and *prime* times to fish.

Rainbow trout have the stuff from which flyfishing "bums" are made. The author admits to being one. Fenton Roskelley, pictured here, one of the author's long-time fishing companions, admits to being an outdoor writer. But put a fly rod in his hand on a steelhead river and you'll soon discover why he's recognized as a leading authority on that fishing!

Staying on top of the action also is part of the strategy, and a short chapter is devoted to setting up your own network for flyfishing information.

Planning strategy is aimed mainly at *locating* the fish and determining optimum times to fish for them. *Catching* them includes such tactics as selecting effective fly patterns, rigging tackle properly, and presenting the flies enticingly. All this and more is covered in this book.

I believe my approach to rainbow and steelhead fly fishing makes a lot of sense, and I hope it helps you find more action wherever you seek these superb game fish.

1

Getting to Know Rainbows and Steelheads

There was a certain presence about the middle-aged man who ambled over to chat before stepping into the river. It could be felt in the rocky firmness of his handshake, observed in the quietly alert gray eyes. As he talked with us about the generally poor steelhead fishing there'd been, and why it had been so, one got the feeling he was very much in tune with the rhythms of that river and those of the few fish trickling upstream.

Talking with him, one felt that if anyone on the river that evening could assess where and when the fish might start moving, this fellow would surely be the one.

His ways, clothing, and tackle contrasted sharply with the more nattily equipped anglers who had gathered to flyfish at last light. They stood about in small groups, sipping coffee, talking

quietly. But their eyes were on each other. His were on the river.

Admittedly, his fly reel had come from a garage sale. The wraps on his fly rod were frayed, the guides, heavily scored from repeated casting, were sorely in need of repair. His waders were stained, yellowing, cut in the baggy manner of a vintage soon to be forgotten, felt soles worn hazardously thin. And his hat was of a style preferred mainly by working cattlemen, the inner sweatband darkly stained, the base of the crown circled only by a thin, simply knotted thong.

The man's utter simplicity of dress and demeanor reminded me of the first fly fishermen I had encountered on this great river, when only a few had been aware of its then superb fly fishing for sea-run rainbow trout. He reminded me of them, men and women to whom fly

He reminded me of . . . men and women . . . to whom the fly rod seemed more an extension of the personality, than an implement.

fishing was a lifestyle rather than a fleeting recreation; to whom the fly rod seemed more an extension of the personality than an implement.

I looked away, thinking of this, then at my watch. It was time to start fishing. But already he was moving unobtrusively down the bank towards the river's edge. And as he moved effortlessly into the water, that presence detected earlier came into clearer focus. His straight casts probed each vagary of current in relentless search for the quarry.

Then, suddenly, his rod bent, its tip bucking as a surprised steelhead tried to rid itself of the hook. There was no stumbling, splashing race to shore to chase down a fish not yet committed to a run. There were no frenetic shouts of "fish on!"

He turned my way, and I thought I detected a grin. He muttered "nice fish," and I knew it was. Soon, he led the fish to the beach. Within moments, he disappeared around a bend in the river.

The rest of us fishing there, I suppose a half-dozen, may have felt pangs of envy, for the unassuming, drably equipped visitor had done what he had done so effortlessly. He left us with the impression that he could repeat the act almost any time he wanted.

Let's analyze this angler's tactics. He had chosen to fish one of the only two drifts in a forty-mile stretch of river that had produced any steelhead in nearly a week.

He seemed to know just when to start fishing. The drift was empty of anglers when we were chatting with him. But he knew that the first angler to fish through a stretch of water once the fish start moving usually catches the fish. Either he'd fished the drift many times before,

or he read steelhead water extremely well. His relatively short casts close to shore indicated he knew where the fish moved through this drift. He also seemed to know that a particular 30-foot portion of the run was a hotspot for moving fish, probably because of a slight depression in the stream bed that caused them to hold there momentarily. Both his strategic approach to the water and his execution were flawless. They flowed from his deep understanding of the fish and the river.

In this chapter we'll examine the habits of rainbow trout and steelheads. Through an understanding of their behavior, we can develop an overall flyfishing strategy. Every fish's behavior is determined by its instinctive drives. All the trouts are preoccupied with fulfilling their needs for reproduction, oxygen, food, and protection. How each species pursues these needs differs slightly from the others.

Although the rainbow is classified as a cold-water species, its most *aggressive* feeding takes place in water temperatures above 50 degrees F. In the rainbow's original range, this condition was prevalent. It is native to the fast-flowing, cool-running rivers of western North America that flow into the Pacific Ocean. In past times, all rainbows are thought to have been migrants to the sea, feeding actively there for a year or two, then returning to the stream where they were spawned to reproduce. It was undoubtedly this way for many thousands of years. And there is little doubt that the rainbow's migratory life cycle was well-understood by the Indians of the Pacific Coast who included the fish in their seasonal food-gathering.

Once American sport fishermen came

One of the rainbow's most appreciated qualities is its ability to adapt to so wide a variety of habitats. This fine Kamloops-strain rainbow was taken by the author from a small lake in the interior of British Columbia.

on the scene, however, these stout-hearted trout were introduced into waters with no access to the sea. It was soon learned that the rainbow can adapt itself to an incredibly wide variety of conditions in both still and moving waters. It is also relatively easy to rear in hatcheries.

Thus began what would be the rainbow trout's eastward "migration." Rainbows were shipped to Michigan in 1873. This was followed in 1874 and 1875 by

Although the rainbow is classified as a cold-water species, its most aggressive feeding takes place in water temperatures above 50 degrees F. This 15-pound summer-run steelhead was taken from Idaho's Clearwater River when the water temperature was approximately 56 degrees.

trips to New York State. Rainbow stock from Campbell's Creek on the McCloud River in California were shipped for experimental transplant to eastern waters. These were reared at Seth Green's Caledonia Hatchery. And in the decade to follow, nine million of their offspring were introduced into the northeastern states and Canada. Since then, the fish has been spread artificially throughout much of the United States and Canada, and to suitable waters in Europe, South America, and the old British Empire. Today, the fish is at home from Alaska to the Andes; from the Revelstoke plateau in British Columbia to the Appalachians; from the highest alpine meadows and tumbling rills, to the deepest desert canyons. These varied habitats differ, of course, and influence the rainbow's spawning and feeding habits.

Reproduction

Truly wild strains of rainbow trout, both sea-going and landlocked, are *spring* spawners. The spawning cycles of some hatchery-bred rainbows have been altered intentionally to produce larger offspring or to extend their stay in lake or ocean prior to spawning. Others have been bred selectively to grow larger more quickly. Yet, all this has little effect on fishing for them, only on seasonal strategies. Under the scales, they're all rainbows.

What is important to understand is that for even wild rainbows "spring" is relative to the region. They spawn today in the varied springtimes of a now greatly expanded and more diversified range. To the present-day rainbow, spring depends on elevation, ice-out time, angle of sunlight, water tempera-

ture, and the other variables affecting aquatic seasons.

In North America, this means sometime between February and July. The northern-tier states, Canadian provinces, and Alaska all have more prolonged winter seasons than the Southeast and Southwest. As a result, it often comes as a surprise to someone from, say, Arkansas, that Alaskan rainbows finning in streams around Bristol Bay may just be emerging from spawning gravel by early July.

Such late aquatic springtimes come as less of a surprise to anglers frequenting the Upper Peninsula of Michigan, the eastern California Sierras, or the Tetons in Wyoming. Like the Alaskan rainbows, those fish may also wear their dark spawning "dress" well into July.

This contrasts sharply with habitually milder lowland climates, or those having belts of warmer climate within the chillier region. In these, rainbow spawning may commence as early as January. More commonly it takes place beginning in February or March and is pretty much completed by the opening of trout season in April or May.

Generally speaking, the rainbow's spawning cycle begins with ice-out. Some years the ice may last well into May or June, depending on the severity of the winter.

Wild strains of steelheads, both ocean- and lake-run, are mostly spring spawners. Some ocean-run fish move from salt water to fresh water in the winter, between December and March. These are the ones referred to by western anglers as "winter-runs." They refer to steelheads arriving in the river during the spring, summer, and early fall months as "summer-run" steelheads. Some rivers

To the present-day rainbow, spring depends on elevation, ice-out time, and other variables affecting its expanded range.

have runs of both. Each river has its own timetable governing their arrival.

Great Lakes steelheads, referred to by some as "lake fish," also vary greatly in their river arrivals. On the North Shore of Lake Superior, for example, the fish begin to arrive in mid-April, with eighty percent of the run completed by May 20. On other North Shore streams, spawning activity occurs as late as July. Steelheads in other streams, such as Wisconsin's

Brule River, enter in the fall and remain over the winter months. In Lake Huron, on the other hand, two runs, one spawning in the winter, the other during early spring, have been reported. In still others, fall runs also occur, but, in Lake Superior, these fish often return to the lake before freeze-up. The Au Sable River in Michigan was the first Great Lakes stream to receive rainbows, when fish from the Northville Hatchery were

planted there in 1876. Since the intro-
duction of Coho and Chinook salmon
into the Great Lakes, some of the better
fly fishing now occurs in fall and early
winter when the opportunistic steelheads follow the spawning salmon to
feed on their dropped eggs. Experiments
are presently underway by several states
to determine if a true Great Lakes
summer run can be created with the
Skamania strain imported from Washington state.

Although the majority of steelheads
spawn in the spring, there's a significant
difference in the timing of the spawning
in ocean-run fish. Winter-run steelheads
head for the redds almost immediately
after entering the river. Summer-run
steelies linger in the river through the
winter months, spawning in the spring
following their arrival. To catch them on
flies, it is essential to fish when they are
in the river. Arrive too soon, and the fish
simply won't be there. Arrive too late,
when the fish are actually on the redds,
and you'll have poorer sport than when
the fish are moving upriver.

Even though there are predictable
times for fish arrival, delays tend to occur, in fresh water mainly due to ice-out
time, in salt water to other factors.
Quirks of nature, such as drought and
man's need for water and hydroelectric
power, all may come into play and affect
the timing of the run.

In some rivers, steelheads may arrive
on time off the river's confluence with
the Pacific Ocean, only to find the river
mouth blocked by sandbars at the estuarine entrance. In these instances, fall or
winter rains may not have arrived in time
to flush a fish passage through the sandbars at the river's mouth. Encountering
this, the steelheads have little choice

other than to await the rains or wend
their ways up another nearby river having open access to the sea. Interestingly,
a small percentage of each river's native
steelheads opts to spawn in a river other
than that in which they were spawned.
In this manner, it seems that nature provides that urge to assure the species' survival.

An unusual condition referred to as a
"thermal block" also may delay the arrival of the steelheads. Thermal blocks
sometimes arise when the water temperature flowing from a spawning tributary is significantly warmer than that of
the river into which it flows. When this
coincides with steelhead arrival at the
tributary mouth, the fish sometimes
linger there until well after suitable *flyfishing conditions* in the tributary have
ended. It is a condition affecting summer
runs.

Steelheads also may linger in pools behind dams. In drought years especially,
the dam's pool may be more comfortably cool for the fish than the river up
which they'd be migrating under normal
water conditions.

In the case of summer-run fish, the
steelheads' departure from the dam's
pool may not occur until shortly before
the fish must surge upstream to satisfy
the spawning urge. By this time, they
may no longer be in prime condition.
They can be caught on flies then, but
their fighting ability has so declined that
it is scarcely worth the bother of fishing
for them.

These kinds of interference with steelhead runs occur often enough to warrant
careful tracking of the fishes' upriver
progress, beginning soon after they enter
fresh water. I will discuss this in a later
chapter.

Although many western flyfishers, including the author, question whether strictly freshwater-bound steelheads are really "steelheads," there is little or no evidence to the contrary. The Great Lakes rainbows mainly stem from the Chamber's Creek steelhead strain and others equally "steelhead" in origin.

For the lake fish, the lake plays a role similar to that of the ocean in the life cycle of western steelheads. There the fish forage actively, attaining impressive size and weight. Their fighting qualities are certainly "close to par," in my opinion, to those of ocean-run fish.

Rainbow spawning behavior in other landlocked, free-flowing streams differs in varying degrees from that of lake fish. Spring-creek rainbows may need to "run" only a few yards to reach suitable gravel to spawn; others in larger streams may need to run a bit farther to gravelly channels or smaller tributary streams.

Rainbows cannot spawn successfully in lakes lacking suitable tributary streams. The eggs require a certain amount of agitation for fertilization and hatching to occur. A flow of current over the eggs also is needed to prevent them being silted over. But the rainbows don't know that. All they're aware of is the urgency to drop the eggs and envelop them in a cloud of milt. So they go through the motions anyway. Since this

Rainbows spawn unsuccessfully in lakes lacking suitable tributaries. But the rainbows don't know that and go through the motions anyway. At that time they are extremely vulnerable to both winged predators and those having arms, legs, and fly rods.

usually takes place in very shallow water in lakes, the fish are exceedingly vulnerable to both winged predators and fishermen.

Still waters, managed exclusively as trout fisheries, may provide some of the better flyfishing opportunities in a region, aside from spawning season. Some are regulated to assure the survival of all the fish, or at least a significant proportion of the larger trout. At lower elevations, such lakes afford unusually fine fly fishing in the spring, fall and, sometimes, winter seasons.

Feeding Behavior

One of the reasons the rainbow trout is so highly adaptable to varying habitats is its willingness to feed on practically anything that swims in fresh water. If something looks edible to the rainbow, it's more than likely the fish will chase it down, root it loose, or grub it out and eat it. Propriety forbids mentioning some items I've found in rainbow trout stomachs. These omniverous feeding habits determine flyfishing tactics.

If rainbow trout were as wary and nocturnal as brown trout, fishing for them surely would be far more difficult. On a trout-catching difficulty scale of 5, rainbows would rank about number 2, second only to the easily duped brook trout, which really isn't a trout at all but a char.

In the broadest sense, the rainbow trout has a troutlike diet. Until reaching a length of about a foot, it concentrates mainly on small aquatic insects, crustaceans, and annelids. Later, it shifts to a meatier diet consisting of large and small insects, crustaceans, annelids, and forage fishes. In this respect, the rainbow differs little from brook, brown, or cutthroat trout. Rainbows do differ from the other trouts in the ways they take artificial flies, their prompt recovery from fright, and their tendency to cluster when migrating or feeding.

How Rainbows Take a Fly

Rainbow trout have a speed advantage over the other trouts. If a rainbow wants to race a brown or cutt to a morsel, it's an eight-to-five chance the rainbow will win the race.

Because the rainbow has this advantage and prefers well-oxygenated water, it will often be found feeding in swifter currents than the other trouts. But not always. Like the other trouts, rainbows tend to *move* to where food is abundant. This is true in both lakes and streams. Their speed gives the rainbows a distinct advantage over other species in chasing down fast-moving forage fish or aquatic insects, like the nymphs of the dragonfly. When rainbows are in the chasing mood, their strikes tend to be very solid and aggressive. Sometimes they are solid enough to part the leader.

Rainbows tend to be more deliberate when feeding on such slow-moving creatures as shrimps, midges, and mayflies, and will quickly and delicately accept or reject the artificial.

With few exceptions, the most determined strikes from rainbows and steelheads (and for browns to a lesser extent) occur once the fly has swung directly below your casting position and come to rest in the current. If the current is moving along at a good clip, say five miles per hour, the rod tip may be yanked completely into the water when the fish grabs the fly and turns downstream. Before the fly begins its cross-current sweep, you'll rarely feel a hard tug.

If you're fishing a nymph, wet fly, or bucktail across stream, you may see the leader hesitate and feel resistance at the end of the tippet. If you're fishing a dry fly, the more slowly the water is moving, the more deliberate the take tends to be. Artificials suggesting leeches may be hit aggressively in strong, deep current; far more gently in still or slowly moving waters.

There is considerable variation also in the way rainbows capture a fly floating on or swimming in the surface film. In fast currents, the takes most often are quick and determined. In slow-moving currents, the rise-form often is more deliberate and slower-paced, such as a head-and-tail type of rise. Dry caddisflies skittered across the surface, on the other hand, may be met with a deeply swirling rise, in which the trout first drowns the caddis, then turns underwater to take it in.

Attempting to attract rainbows to artificials resembling adult damselflies is even more frustrating. The fish usually capture the adult insects while they are climbing up stems of water plants, or hovering *above* the surface. Once the hatch has concluded, the rainbows look above the surface to find them. Strikes on spent-wing damsel artificials are often few and far between, but splashy when they do occur. The infrequency of strikes tends to lull you into complacency; when a strike does occur you may overreact and break your tippet.

Steelheads rarely come well to the fly in water moving along much faster than an angler can walk. There are exceptions, of course, most often in extremely fast-moving rivers like the North Thomp-

son in British Columbia. There are places where that river churns along like a ten-wheeler out of control on a downhill grade! The current is so powerful that I've had British-made double fly hooks practically straightened by the strike of a heavy fish.

For the most part, however, the steelhead takes a well-sunk, sweeping bucktail fly in the same aggressive way as a resident rainbow attacking a streamer fly. What happens *after* the strike marks the difference between the two fish.

Fishing a wet or dry fly for steelheads through the surface film provides even greater excitement. Sometimes several steelhead will fall in behind the riffled fly and follow it some distance on the cross-stream sweep before one of them hits it. This causes Vs to form in the surface film immediately behind the fly. The anticipation takes your breath away! And although the strike may be impressively powerful and showy, it tends to be anticlimactic.

The take of a steelhead capturing a free-floating dry fly varies little from that of any large, resident rainbow. There's a splash or a swirl. The fly disappears. You lift the rod and a powerful fish surges away, shakes its head, then jumps or runs. If the dry fly has swung into the current, and is waking cross-current in the way of a riffled wet or dry fly, the fish's attack is fierce. Just watching the Vs caused by the fish trailing the fly across stream can bring your heart to your throat. (Classic "crisis.") The strike occasions "lysis."

Recovery from Fright

Rainbows recover quickly from being frightened. I recall one 18-incher I tried to hustle too quickly from the Firehole River in Yellowstone Park. I'd hooked the fish on a size 14 Hare's Ear Nymph in the Bisquit Basin stretch. Excessive haste in playing the fish cost me both fish and fly. Returning to the same run several hours later, I hooked and released the same fish, which to my surprise, had retained my barbless nymph in its lip all that time.

Once my son Bill and I were fishing a small river in Colorado. It had been blocked by a 40-foot-high concrete dam to form a lake. Grasshoppers were everywhere. But strong breezes prompted us to start fishing below the dam where a jackpine woods blocked some of the wind.

The surface of the dam was alive with hopping hoppers. There were so many grasshoppers that many were being blown into the concrete-lined catch-basin at the base of the dam. We looked down and thrilled to the sight of numerous large rainbow trout cruising the catch-basin pool, plucking hapless hoppers from the surface.

My son was so excited by this that he half ran, half tumbled down the steep dirt path leading to the pool forty feet below, making a lot of commotion. Most of the 12- to 20-inch rainbows gathered in the pool stopped feeding immediately.

But within five minutes, some of the trout resumed feeding, plucking struggling hoppers from the surface. Nevertheless, I cautioned Bill to let the pool rest another ten minutes. When he resumed fishing, his first six casts produced five thrashing, jumping trout. Fortunately for my son, all were too dumb to race downstream from the pool. He landed and released all, before the commotion again slowed the feeding activity.

But the story's not over. I sent him downstream to test his skills on some trout I'd spotted rising to caddis in an eddy. I sat down and smoked a cigarette, keeping one eye on Bill, the other on the catch-basin pool. Within ten minutes, a half-dozen trout were again feeding on hoppers. I hooked and landed two of them in the 14- to 16-inch class. Downstream, Bill caught browns feeding on caddis emergers.

Feeding in Clusters

Some trout, especially large brown trout, tend to be relatively solitary in their feeding habits. Rainbow trout, on the other hand, like to feed in the company of their kind. Fish of similar size and age tend to stay together.

The rainbow gathering is a predictable phenomenon, but it occurs in different ways. Sometimes they'll feed over an extensive expanse of water, such as a large bay in a lake. Yet, on small trout streams, such as Water's Creek in northern Georgia, only a half-dozen fish drift from cover towards the center of a pool to meet an evening hatch. On large streams, such as the Yellowstone in Montana, the rainbows may accumulate to feed right along with brown trout, cutthroats, and whitefish when food in a certain location becomes abundant.

Being keenly aware of the rainbow's tendency to feed in a group has influenced my fishing tactics. Today, when I go fishing *specifically* for rainbow trout, I often travel quickly from one area of the lake or stream to another, seeking concentrations of actively feeding fish.

With migrating steelheads, my strategy is similar, because of the fish's tendency to move upriver in groups of varying

Steelheads migrate in pods on their spawning runs. These summer-run fish were caught in the fall from a pod of steelheads that had gathered at the mouth of their spawning tributary.

size. For I've learned that hooking a fish or seeing one roll indicates there are other steelheads in the vicinity.

Feeding Moods and Movements in Lakes

Several factors affect a rainbow's behavior in lakes. Perhaps the most generally recognized of these, amongst fly fishermen, is water temperature. As indicated in the early part of this chapter, the rainbow's most aggressive feeding occurs in a temperature range above 50 degrees Fahrenheit—in my experience, from 55 to 65 degrees. Maximum lake insect movement and hatching also occur at these temperatures. Extreme variations from this range often cause the trout to head for parts of the lake where temperatures are closer to their preference. To a certain extent, this knowledge helps you and me to zone in on lake rainbows with fair accuracy from season to season.

Recent research into fish behavior, however, indicates reading of the water temperatures that rainbows prefer is less productive than evaluating other water conditions that more directly affect their *willingness* to feed. The most reliable measurement, according to the researchers, is of the water's pH, the acid-base relationship existing in the water. (pH is now measurable with compact, dependable instruments.) Investigating the effects of pH and some other factors, such as water clarity, may lead to a greater understanding of why trout become difficult to locate or seemingly go off their feed.

Practically speaking, we can look upon pH as similarly affecting all species of freshwater game fish. Fish, like human beings, have a blood pH of 7.4. (The pH measurement scale runs from 1 to 14, with 7 being the "neutral" point. Anything below 7 is acidic, above 7 alkaline.) But fish live in a far different medium than we do. They get their oxygen from the water. Even minor changes in water pH affect the ability of fish to extract oxygen from it. Under suitable pH conditions fish can get the oxygen they need from relatively oxygen-starved water. But if the pH is too high or too low, they can't get enough oxygen even from water that is oxygen-rich.

New research indicates that fish are most active in water having a pH ranging from 7.5 to 8.5 and that they'll continue to be active and aggressive in water with a pH between 7 and 9. Above or below that range, fish are difficult to find and hard to catch.

One reason this information is so useful in understanding rainbow trout behavior in lakes is because so much of their prime seasonal feeding takes place on the lake's shallow, weedy food shelf. Sunlight-induced photosynthesis causes radical changes in pH in these weedy areas during the prime times of year for fly fishing.

Sunlight causes water plants to extract carbon dioxide from the water and to return oxygen and calcium carbonate into it. When this occurs, the pH in that part of the lake goes up rapidly. When the pH passes the comfortable limit for the trout, they move elsewhere. This explains why flyfishers finding weedy shallows full of feeding trout during early morning and late evening hours often find those same weed beds barren of trout at midday. Because large fish are more affected by a pH change than small fish, it also explains why trout caught from weedy areas during the heat of the day tend to be small.

Sunlight also causes algae and plankton to photosynthesize and multiply. Often, this runs the pH up past the trout's comfort range over large areas of the lake, sometimes throughout the entire lake. As a result, when the "bloom" of the algae or plankton becomes dense at or near the surface, the rainbows usually seek deeper water. This means a sinking fly line is needed to reach that deeper lake zone where the trout have moved.

The pH varies seasonally. During winter, lake pH tends to stabilize because the sun is lower, the water is colder, algae and plankton are dormant, plantlife is "down," and there is less or no runoff through fertilized fields or over limestone rock formations.

In spring, rains wash nutrients and silt into the lake. Because the lake water is cold and the rain is warmer, the less dense runoff flows out over the lake's surface, causing its muddy appearance during that time of year. This causes a clarity layering.

The opposite occurs in the summer, when water temperatures are reversed. Then, the surface waters clear. Cooler rain sinks below the warmer surface layer, causing a murky layer to form underneath it.

Transitional zones form between layers. Rainbows and other predator fishes are likely to concentrate in the vicinity of these "breaklines."

In the case of the pH breakline, the trout may be attracted to photosynthesizing zooplankton. Forage fish feed on the zooplankters. Rainbows feed on forage fishes.

In the case of the clarity layering, the more turbid layer may serve as camouflage for predatory rainbows to conceal themselves from forage fish swimming by in the clearer layer.

Thus, in seeking probable locations of lake rainbows, it is most logical to first seek out areas having ideal pH, for that is where the fish are likely to be the most aggressive. Lacking a pH meter, the next choice is to look for changes in water clarity, for aggressive fish may lurk in the camouflage. The third most reliable approach is to identify lake zones having temperatures that encourage feeding.

Feeding in Fast Water

One of the more significant differences between the species of trouts is in the various speeds of current each seems to prefer. The rainbow's preference is for well-oxygenated, relatively fast-flowing currents. The well-oxygenated waters are where they feed the most aggressively.

There are some qualifications to this statement, of course. It has been my experience that rainbows rarely go on the prowl in currents racing along two or three times faster than a person can walk. You must remember that the topwaters of the stream often flow significantly faster than those down deep. Thus, in a fast, deep run having a stream bed consisting of boulders, the boulders may sufficiently disperse current along the bottom to provide holding lies for the trout. Large boulders in rapids play a similar role in creating suitable lies for 'bows.

During the brightest daylight hours, it's common for rainbows in fast-flowing streams to move to a "protective" combination of currents that conceal them

Well-oxygenated waters, like this, are where rainbows feed most aggressively.

In some streams, such as the Gallatin River in Montana, large boulders provide sufficient breaks in the current to attract rainbows.

from predators above, but that allow some opportunities to feed. The old-time flyfishing writers referred to such currents as "broken" water.

On a small, Catskill stream, this may simply be where a riffle bubbles into a deeper pool.

On an even slower-moving spring creek, this may be where the flow merely roughens ever so slightly over gravel, weed, or rock.

Wherever rainbows are found in large-sized streams or rivers, "rock" very often indicates their presence nearby. In some, bowling-ball-sized boulders lying at the juncture of pool and rapids attract the rainbows. The most attractive of

these rocky lies to rainbows frequently are located near more exposed, less broken currents such as eddies.

Riffles of slow to moderate speed are among the best for rainbows. And one stretch of a large trout stream comes particularly to mind.

The stretch in question consists of a moderately swift riffle, ranging from a foot to four feet deep. The overall length of the riffling water is about a quarter mile, which then sweeps into a very deep, fast run downstream.

The entire riffle is well-distributed with good-sized boulders from midstream to both shorelines. There's a deep slot on the lower far side of the riffle.

In spring creeks, rainbows often feed where the stream flow quickens, such as a shallower run flowing into a pool, as in this stretch of Armstrong Spring Creek in Montana.

Deciduous oak and live oak, and a lot of dense willows border both banks. These shade the deep slot on the far side of the riffle as well as the slow-moving waters on the other side.

In late spring, patches of water weeds appear throughout the riffle. These trail in the current near the surface, making across stream presentations difficult.

Stream-bed depressions form a stair-step effect every fifty yards or so down through the riffle.

When stonefly and caddisfly hatches are in full swing, you can virtually count on finding the rainbows dispersed throughout the riffle, along the breakline

leading to the deeper slot, and along a breakline leading to a slower-moving slot at the head of the riffle.

When the insects are not actively crawling about or hatching, the rainbows move to the cross-stream depressions, podding up under the broken water. And when this happens, concentrating on those pockets produces strikes. Often, fish can be taken from the riffle all day long.

The broken water formed by the meeting of different speeds of current plays an extremely important role for rainbows feeding in the stream. (The old-time writers referred to these as current "edges." Now we often refer to them as "seams.") For drifting natural trout foods tend to accumulate where the faster-moving currents meet slower ones. Rainbows often cluster along them when plenty of drifting food is coming by.

Some of the better kinds of current edges are formed by the configuration of the stream bank (such as ox-bow bends), by stream-bed depressions or bars, and by weed growth. Boulders or fallen trees also create similar seams in the current.

Both rainbows and browns feed in the slower currents of the eddys, inhaling submerged morsels and sipping floating naturals from the surface. Rainbows can be found in the shallower eddys almost anytime; browns feed there when a hatch is in progress or at night and on overcast days. Eddys next to undercut banks are even more to browns' liking.

One of the more productive kinds of eddy in which to seek rainbow trout is where rapids churn around a bend in the river, forming eddying currents off to one side. If the nearby rapids contain large boulders attractive to rainbows, not only a considerable number of trout, but also some large ones may prowl the area.

Think of the rapids, the eddy, and the run-and-pool sequence as a virtual "magic triangle" for rainbow trout. The eddy is most likely to be the rainbows' main feeding station during a hatch or spinnerfall. The boulders in the rapids

The current "edges" tend to accumulate food drifting downstream.

are likely to be where the fish retreat for protection.

Rainbows tend to linger in eddies. Some fish hold there most of the time, especially the smaller 'bows. Therefore, the fishing sequence should begin with the near-shore eddy, progress outward to the fast water, then downstream into the run and pool.

In approaching the eddy lying near an exposed shore, it pays to remain well back from the water while making the first few casts into it. Sneaking up on hands and knees is a sound tactic. But before casting, try to determine if the trout are holding or feeding. If no surface feeding is underway, offer your flies within the eddy *first*. Then gradually ex-

tend your casts to fish the outer current-seam. This way you won't "line" the fish.

Very early in the morning and late in the evening it's common for the rainbows (browns, too!) to move to slower, shallower parts of the river to feed. Sometimes their shallow-water quarry will be immature trout and forage fish that find safety there most of the time. Other times, it will be varieties of caddis and mayflies that hatch from quieter waters. If the river bottom there is rocky, there's a good likelihood of the fish seeking out crayfish, as well.

Some of the best such locations are side channels. At midday, you might expect these to harbor cutthroat trout feed-

On large rivers, such as this one, the author looks for sequences of rapids, runs, riffles, pools, and side channels in close proximity to one another.

ing on caddis, mayflies and terrestrials. In the West, five out of six "channel" fish may be whitefish.

Rainbows in Low Water Conditions

Rainbow trout seem to require more oxygen than brown trout. In late summer low water conditions rainbows may be comfortable only in well-oxygenated riffles, rapids, and where rapids churn into runs and pools.

I recall a day on the Kalama River in southwestern Washington state, when large pods of steelheads accumulated in riffles scarcely deep enough to cover their backs. Discovering this while wading across such a riffle, my companions and I hooked several fish from lies we would have completely bypassed under normal water conditions.

Steelhead Behavior

The large size and superb fighting qualities of steelheads tend to override the fact that the fish are rarely caught in large numbers. Despite the fact that steelheads are among the easiest of rainbows to bring to the fly under ideal water conditions, the relatively small number of fish constituting spawning runs limits one's expectations. In this way, steelhead fishing more resembles hunting than fishing.

Ideal flyfishing conditions for steelheads are those under which they tend to be most *aggressive* in coming to the fly. For summer-run fish these usually include clear or slightly tinted rising waters ranging in temperature from 55 to 65 degrees F. For winter-run steelheads, the ideal temperatures range about ten degrees colder.

Problems associated with catching summer-run steelies at that 55 to 65 degree range rarely involve coaxing the fish to come to the fly. In this respect they're far less annoying than Atlantic salmon. If you put the fly where a steelhead can see it, it will usually come for it with determination. Steelheads under these conditions will freely rise to take in a floating dry fly or riffled wet fly or bucktail. And they will do this as aggressively as they might race to capture a fly worked close to the river bottom.

Winter-run steelheads tend to be the most aggressive for a brief period of time after entering fresh water. The *first* drift above a steelhead river's tide-line often will be the most consistently productive one for fly fishermen.

Sometimes, fly fishers engage steelheads with flies while the fish are still lingering in the estuary. Some anglers feel that the fish actually do feed until the onset of sexual maturation forces them to head for the redds. Some Great Lakes runs come on the heels of salmon runs. There, the steelheads are believed to feed upon eggs dropped by the spawning salmon.

Professional steelhead/salmon guide J. D. Love of Beaver, Washington, feels that the optimum winter-run flyfishing water temperatures on the Olympic Peninsula rivers range upwards from 44 degrees F. However, such cold waters do not prompt winter-run fish to move far to greet the fly. For winter fly fishing the Great Lakes tributaries, fast-sinking sink-tip and shooting-taper lines rigged with four- to six-foot leaders are needed to sweep the fly close to the fishes' noses. Great persistence is needed to prompt strikes, far greater than when fishing for the highly aggressive summer-run steelies.

Ideal water temperatures for summer-run steelhead fishing range between 55 and 65 degrees Fahrenheit. The water temperature where this wader tied into a nice one in the Snake River in Washington state was 55 degrees.

Steelhead Feeding

There is sufficient evidence to indicate that both winter- and summer-run steelheads may feed for a time while acclimatizing to fresh water in tidally affected parts of western rivers. However, there is little to suggest they actually ingest, or are even capable of ingesting foods as the time for reproduction approaches.

I have caught numerous summer-run steelheads having grasshoppers in their mouths and throats. Some also have taken in caddisflies. And over the years I have killed and dressed enough steelheads to be convinced actual feeding does *not* take place far from the estuarine reaches of the rivers. Not one of the steelheads I have examined had a morsel of natural trout food in its stomach. This sampling consists of over a hundred steelheads caught since the mid-1950s. The larger proportion of steelheads I've caught were released unharmed.

Some anglers believe that the steelheads continue to capture aquatic and terrestrial insects, or take salmon eggs into their mouths because of latent, instinctive "memory" of having done so as parr, smolts, or first-time returnees to the river. Whether that is true or not has little bearing on the fly fishing.

I recall an early October day in the 1970s when a friend "borrowed" a half-dozen large Bivisibles from me to fish extremely low, clear summer-run stream conditions. The water temperature was about 65 degrees F., due to unseasonably hot weather. The river had risen a bit overnight. But the water was only lightly stained.

"You're not going to believe this," he exclaimed as he trudged into the camp area while I was building a cooking fire. "I've just had the best day of steelhead fly fishing of my life! All of the fish came to your Bivisibles! What do you think of that!"

"Great," said I, "How many fish? A dozen or so?"

"Nope," said he, "How does over 30 fish sound?"

"Like a grandiose exaggeration!" I grinned, setting the coffee pot on a hot rock by the roaring fire.

My friend didn't smile. In fact he looked like I might have hurt his feelings. "Have you ever known me to lie?" he said soberly. I hadn't.

"Rex, I lost count at thirty hookups. Honest to gosh! I must have hit another half-dozen fish after that." I believed him.

When steelheads are heavily podded up in holding lies, or when steadily moving from pool to pool throughout the river, such a fishing day can occur. I've experienced a few of them myself. There is always the remote possibility of en-

countering enough aggressive summer-run fish to produce that sort of day.

Entering the River

Both tidal effects and current flow affect the fly fishing in the reaches of steelhead streams close to the ocean. Often the three- or four-hour period following a high tide may find steelheads bright from the salt-chuck moving into the lower drifts of the river. At times, these fish are highly aggressive. At other times they're not. The aggressive fish most often seem to move into relatively shallow riffles and runs which are accessible to flyfishing tactics. But when the river's cold and roily, the fish may be prompted to move into deeper stretches where it is difficult to catch them on anything except bait.

Once the steelheads move upstream past the influences of tidal flows, they tend to move on rising waters, and to hold when the water is cooling down and falling. This upstream movement often follows currents adjacent to, but not directly in the fastest current. Like resident rainbows, then, steelheads gravitate to seams in the current, but in this instance not for the same reason.

Steelhead Traveling

Fish and game department tracking studies of migrating steelheads indicate the fish do most of their upstream movement at night, or on dark overcast days. The studies also indicate that some of the fish may travel as far as twenty-five miles a day.

Interestingly, the nightime movements of steelheads do not appear to include difficult stretches of rapids. To move along through these, they seem to require better visibility.

Some types of water in which I have repeatedly connected with moving steelheads include long, rocky riffles and runs—and, in very early morning, runs leading into rapids in which the fish need visibility to navigate. There are others, of course, and we'll get into all that later.

It was in a run leading into a rapids I enjoyed one of my most productive mornings of summer-run steelhead fishing. My two friends and I hooked and released forty-two steelheads there in a three-hour period. What was most interesting about the fishing that morning was that virtually all of the fish were

taken on small, size 10 flies! Skunks, Silver Ants, Rogue River Specials, and Red Ants as I recall.

Steelhead Holding

Migrating fish, like steelheads, need to pause in their travels and rest periodically. Oftentimes, this "holding pattern" will occur at the top of a long stretch of rapids the fish have ascended during daylight hours.

It is important to recognize the time of day when they've moved into such a location. Over a thirty-year period, I've found this usually to be well after they've swum up the rapids in the early morning hours. Such holding lies nor-

"Tailing-out" currents leading from a rapids into a run are ideal locations to find "traveling" steelheads working upstream along the current edges.

Ideal steelhead holding water often occurs near the upstream brink of a rapids—in slower moving water having large boulder formations. This one has produced summer-run steelheads for the author since the mid-1950's.

mally contain fish anytime from mid-morning to early evening. Ideal locations seem most often to occur near the brink of the rapids, where slower currents flow over large boulders in three to eight feet of water.

The pattern's often different for winter-run fish and for summer-run steelheads seeking respite from cold water. At these times, the most preferred holding lies often will occur in the lower, slower-moving reaches of pools not necessarily associated with rapids immediately downstream.

The colder the water, the more dogged your persistence may need to be to coax holding steelheads into action. Take a chilly February afternoon when the water temperature rested at 42 degrees F. as a good example.

Fish had been moving steadily upstream until the water temperature took a nose-dive. We opted to fish a slow-moving pool a few hundred yards upstream from a churning rapids. The river bottom here was honeycombed with channels in the slippery ledgerock. I suggested my companion fish through the drift first, since he'd had less time on the water than I that season.

He fished the "hot spot" in the run doggedly for over an hour. I estimate he made 200 casts through the forty-foot-long channel which normally held fish when they were there.

Once he had moved some distance downstream, I worked a cast into the same slot, hooking a large rock and necessitating a break-off of the fly.

My second cast was greeted with a jolting take. The steelhead, though not a large one, raced downstream and jumped right next to my friend. This so surprised him that he lost his balance and fell in!

As I decided to break off the fish and rush to his assistance, he regained his footing on the treacherous river bottom. Without saying it, we both sensed that his repeated casting had "primed" that steelhead for a response to just one more presentation, which sadly had to be mine.

I felt badly about being the one to make that important final cast. So did he, until he had changed clothing and taken a long pull on a jug of Lurking Turkey.

It was only after a second, hefty slug of Turkey that I sensed he'd forgiven me.

2
Finding Productive Waters

Rainbow trout populations tend to fluctuate from season to season. Spawning success in past years determines the number of wild trout in a lake or stream. Planting cycles, the number of fish introduced, as well as angler success, affect those maintained artificially. In addition, so many other factors affect fishing that even experienced anglers miscalculate in planning their trips.

To avoid such errors, it is necessary to locate productive waters and determine the best times to fish them.

First of all, simply because rainbow trout or steelhead occur in large numbers in a lake or stream is no reason to assume there will be good fly fishing. The other factors that count include the character of the water, available food, and such influences as dam construction, drought, excessively cold winters,

summertime agricultural draw-downs of water, inadvertent spills of toxic materials, fishing pressure, fisheries management practices, competition for food between the trout and other species, and summer- or winter-kills caused by oxygen depletion through natural causes.

In general, lakes and streams that, over a period of time, have produced *consistently good* fly fishing, and that are managed properly so there are abundant large fish, tend to be your best bets. Some of these are located in the more remote regions of the United States and Canada. In these waters, wild trout, light fishing pressure, and conservative management produce top-quality fly fishing. Not everyone can afford to fish these waters, but there are good alternatives.

The more economically accessible alternatives to remote wild rainbow trout

Unpublicized "public" waters, like this little lake in the interior of British Columbia, Canada, often produce rainbow trout fly fishing rivaling that in exotic, far-away locations.

and steelhead fishing are to be found in certain forward-looking states such as Montana. Some of this fishing is on private waters owned by clubs where the high membership fees may exclude those of average means. Other public lakes and streams may offer fishing of a quality equal to the private waters because of having had little or no publicity. Others are simply *managed* to yield excellent fishing for larger-than-average 'bows. Identifying this latter group of quality waters is as easy as reading the fine print in the state or province's published sportfishing regulations pamphlets. In most instances, these very special trout fisheries are listed under "Special Regulations." Most often, these refer to restrictions on tackle and catch limits. Those identified as "no kill," "catch and release," "fly fishing only," "artificial lures and flies," and "artificial lures and flies, barbless hooks only," can be considered *prime* flyfishing possibilities for whatever species of trout may exist there.

The unpublicized lakes and streams having good rainbow fly fishing may be more difficult to identify. But it can be accomplished, using investigative methods and a little common sense. The key to it involves developing *reliable* sources of information, which we'll discuss both here and in a later chapter.

There is plenty of information available to fly fishermen, but considerable effort and imagination are needed to gather it. Some may come through well-nurtured personal contacts. Some is available as public record. And some of the best through seminars and lectures offered by flyfishing clubs and tackle shops. It doesn't hurt to be friends with a well-placed, influential "politician" or

two, either, when it comes to determining the construction dates planned for new dams.

Sources of Information

Let's take a closer look at some of the better information sources for the fly fisherman.

The Federation of Flyfishers (FFF) is dedicated to the encouragement of fly fishing as a sport, and to its continuation through sane water-resources management. Hundreds of flyfishing clubs are affiliated with the FFF. They're to be found in practically every region of the United States.

The FFF publishes its own magazine, *The Flyfisher,* which is devoted to providing useful flyfishing information to its members. The organization also conducts an annual national conclave, which is held at a location providing good fly fishing for the registrants. Programs offered at the conclave usually include in-depth examinations of flyfishing possibilities in the area and, sometimes those of other regions.

The Federation of Flyfishers
P.O. Box 1088
West Yellowstone, MT 59758.
Phone: (406) 646-9541

Flyfishing clubs are often the *best* sources of information about your region's lakes and streams. If the members are generally affluent, they also may be a storehouse of information about remote angling waters.

Like the FFF, regional councils of FFF-affiliated clubs sometimes hold regional conclaves offering informative programs about where to go fly fishing. They're normally scheduled across weekends, to allow maximum registration by club members throughout the region.

The clubs themselves also may offer similar programs to spice up their monthly meetings. Some also schedule group "get acquainted" fishing trips to prime flyfishing waters in the area. Virtually all of the clubs publish some sort of newsletter containing periodic reports on fishing by the members.

Flyfishing publications devoted exclusively to fly fishing include *Rod & Reel, Fly Fishing, Fly Fisherman,* and *The Flyfisher* (the FFF publication). In each, from time to time, you will find articles dealing in depth with how to fish a particularly good stream or lake for rainbows. This information should be verified before embarking on a fishing trip. Fishing conditions may have changed since the author wrote the article.

Most *national sporting publications* publish articles their editors consider to be mainly of national interest, regardless of the subject matter. Some, however, do contain regional sections with fishing and hunting information. Read these regional sections regularly; you may find a gem.

Regional fishing and hunting publications usually are either monthly magazines or weekly tabloid-size newspapers. If the editors of a particular regional are at all sensitive to flyfishing readers, spot news and features about fly fishing will occasionally be found there.

Western Outdoors magazine, and its newspaper affiliate, *Western Outdoors News,* are both generous in this regard, since about half of their readers fly fish. The magazine, for which I am the freshwater-angling columnist, also contains a regular column on fly tying. Some other regionals also cover fly fishing, the ex-

tent depending on the degree of interest in their circulation areas.

Both the spot news and where-to-go feature articles in regionals are excellent sources for information. But even though the regional publication may have a shorter gap between the writing and publication than a national magazine, it still pays to verify conditions at recommended sites before fishing there. Murphy's Law also applies to fishing. If anything can go wrong with the fishing between the time you plan a trip and arrive on the water, it usually will. I have developed a corollary to Murphy's Law for the benefit of fly fishermen. I call it Gerlach's Law of Fly Fishing. It simply states: "Murphy was an optimist!"

Many of the major *daily and weekly newspapers* of the last generation published regular, well-informed fishing columns, often written by anglers who were themselves fly fishermen. That's no longer true today. A lot of the better outdoor columns written when I was a young angler have all but disappeared. So have fishing-oriented journalists capable of writing them.

Today, you can consider yourself lucky to live where the daily or weekly newspaper runs a regular fishing column, even luckier if the columnist happens to be a fly fisher. But if you do, then the writer may prepare a special pre-opening-day regional report, pinpointing those waters where the fishing is most likely to be outstanding. These reports often are prepared with the assistance of the local fish and game department fisheries biologist.

Some *fishing guides* are the best sources of flyfishing information available anywhere. Guides may be on certain waters almost every day throughout

Careful scrutiny of a newspaper's weekly fishing reports identified the river from which this nice rainbow was taken.

Fishing guide services know the rivers in their areas like books. The author employs guides, like Mark Daly pictured here, to fish inaccessible areas of rivers.

the season. They're fully informed about the fishing from firsthand experience. *Light Tackle Fishing Guides of North America* by Richard Swan (Clearwater Press, Reno, NV) can help you find reliable guides near unfamiliar waters. You're likely to find a copy in a nearby flyfishing tackle shop.

Fisheries biologists may be the best of all the sources of information. Quite a few of them are fly fishermen. Depending on their dispositions and workloads, some are quite willing to help a visiting angler plan a successful flyfishing trip to their area. When dealing with them, try to be as friendly, brief, and undemanding as possible. Many have crushing work-

loads. Others, especially those who have to accommodate a lot of fishing writers with information, may not want to be bothered at home, at night, by calls from information-hungry anglers. In that case, do not get sore at the biologist. Simply ask for the name and phone number of a local angler who can provide the information you seek. In some instances, the biologist may be highly sensitive to questions from strangers due to political pressures. Give special consideration to these professionals, who do a superb job of creating and maintaining quality fly fishing.

There are *flyfishing tackle shops* located in nearly every prime flyfishing region in the United States or Canada that are run by persons fully informed about the fly fishing in their region. In California, where I live, some shops have extensive information-gathering networks that supply reports on prime rainbow waters all over the world. Some of these fly shops, such as Marriott's Fly Fishing Store in Fullerton, the Fly Shop in Redding, and Fishermen's Spot in Van Nuys, conduct flyfishing schools and seminars. A lot of information can be gleaned from attending these courses. Some shops even have instructor-guides who, for a fee, will take you out on a piece of water and teach you how to fish it. For the beginner, this sort of personal instruction is a worthwhile investment in both time and money.

Filing the Data

Identifying prospective places to fly-fish for rainbows and steelheads is an important part of planning a trip, but there is more to do. The information needs to be filed, updated, and analyzed. The best way to do this is to have a file folder for each lake or stream. Into this file, put any maps you may have purchased or sketched, copies of related fishing "log" pages, published articles about the lake or stream, lists of fly patterns and sizes that produce there, records of fish-planting data, hatching dates of predominant insect life, copies of fishing regulations, and, if you can obtain them, evaluations of trout-management programs prepared by fisheries biologists.

As I write this, I have before me a copy of an evaluation of trophy-regulated fish management on an especially productive western river that has had very little publicity. It contains a history of the special

regulations beginning in 1960, effects of changes in bag and size limits, seven years of creel data, water-flow graphs, records of angler-use, results of electro-shock fish surveys and current stocking data. It even has a chart comparing the catch-rate to the water-flows, a tremendous aid in timing one's fishing. A similar study, also in my file on another river, goes so far as to estimate the percentage of surveyed trout that have been previously hooked by anglers. This second study also has a section entitled "Management Implications." This gives you some idea of how the state's fish biologists plan to manage the fishery in the future.

You may question the need for keeping such elaborate files. "After all," you may say "rainbows and steelheads are fairly gullible and easy to fool with flies." The objective here, of this entire book for that matter, is to help you to be a more *consistent* fisherman. The angler who catches fish consistently usually derives more satisfaction from the sport than one who doesn't. The ineffective flyfisher has to watch his companions enjoy spectacular fishing and then explain to family and friends why he had "bad luck." That alone provides sufficient motivation for improvement. At least it has for me.

The information you have on file is essentially useless until it is analyzed and conclusions are drawn to help you make decisions about *where, when,* and *how* to fish.

Of course, many waters containing rainbows also contain other species, and some of the information you gather may also relate to them. It's important to consider these species also since some tend to compete with rainbows for food and

The fly fisher who increases his ability to connect with large rainbows more often simply derives more satisfaction from the sport than one who doesn't.

Fishing the peak of a brown trout spawning run.

territory. If that is the case, it's helpful to understand how rainbows move in that particular water in order to compete successfully.

"Good grief!" you exclaim. "How many more variables can you inject into this discussion to confuse me and complicate the fishing?"

First off, don't blame me. The variables are there whether we like it or not. Legitimately, you can blame or congratulate the dam builders for the good and bad effects of their works. You can blame those responsible for toxic waste spills. But in all fairness, all you can blame me for is failure to help you understand and deal with the complex-

ity to achieve more consistent flyfishing success.

Interpreting the Data

A useful overall strategy for fishing a particular lake or stream involves drawing conclusions based on the following data:

- The type of lake or stream.
- The competition for food between the trout and other species.
- Seasonal water flows, pH, temperature, and oxygen levels.
- The types of food used by the trout.
- Data on the spawning of native trout

or the planting of hatchery-reared trout.

- Environmental circumstances that may affect fishing.
- Creel-data from the previous season.
- Productive fly patterns.
- Productive flyfishing tactics.

Let's take an imaginary stream called the "Rainbow River" and develop a preliminary strategy for fishing it next season.

Before 1965, The Rainbow River was a silty stream flowing through a spectacular canyon into a prairie. Most of the sauger, catfish, burbot, goldeye, and Cyprinids (a genus of fish including carp, tench, and roach) in the stream had never seen an angler's hook. Then a dam was built across the canyon, trapping much of the river's silt. Now, the water that flowed from the canyon was very different from the water of the original river many miles downstream. It was cooler in the summer and warmer in the winter. It had become a clear stream, a "tailwater" fishery, ideal for trout.

Between 1966 and 1973, 263,000 rainbows were planted. Brown trout also were introduced. The ability of the planted rainbows to spawn successfully was limited. The browns did very well on their own.

A change in management policy ended rainbow plantings in '73, after which natural spawning by wild fish showed marked improvement. By then, of course, the river had gained a national reputation for producing trophy rainbows and browns over 18 inches long. According to electroshocking studies, there are over 9,000 trout per mile in the prime flyfishing stretches. The greatest numbers of rainbows seem to be located in the upper reaches of this water, due to ideal spawning conditions there.

Both water-flow and gas supersaturation problems occur periodically. The gas sometimes causes high mortality in the brown trout. Excessively low water has also caused some mortality. But the fish have rebounded from the effects of both conditions.

Bureau of Reclamation officials are making a greater effort to maintain a regular water flow from the canyon in March and April. A five-year drought in the area has made this difficult, but more normal snow runoff is predicted this coming year.

Angler use has jumped from 11,667 annual man-days to well over 20,000 during the past four years. This year, a new access area was opened which allows drift-boat fishing on an additional 13 miles of productive water. It's assumed this will spread out the fishing pressure for the browns, since they appear to be less concentrated in specific areas than the rainbows. Despite heavy fishing pressure during the peak of the tourist season in August and early September, a high success rate is forecast.

Although abundant fly hatches do occur, the browns and the rainbows seem to prefer annelids (water worms) and forage fish.

The river was closed to public fishing by the Indian tribe through whose reservation it flows between 1973 and 1981. It was reopened after a lengthy series of court battles determined it to be "navigable."

At that time, trophy trout fishing picked up where it left off in '75. But the recent dramatic increase in fishing pressure seriously concerns fisheries managers. Therefore, the catch limit has been reduced to five fish, with only one fish exceeding 18 inches and only one rainbow allowed. These new regulations, which have been in effect since 1985, already show signs of improving the rainbow-to-brown catch ratio.

Although the trout hatched in 1985 are present in great numbers, their size did not reach trophy-class due to a slow growth rate in the exceedingly cold waters that winter. These fish should be trophy class in 1988, when the Rainbow River may provide the best trophy trout fishing in many years.

Now, let's convert this information into a simple, effective strategy for fishing for *rainbows*. You can draw your own conclusions about the browns.

Best time to fish. May through July. Avoid heaviest fishing pressure. Recov-

Broad, seasonal targeting may be adequate on lightly fished, remote waters, such as this fly-in lake. But on waters that are heavily fished, fine-tuning of the strategy may be needed to avoid disappointments.

Fine-tuning the "quick trip" strategy resulted in Allan Rohrer's catching this heavyweight rainbow from a large spring creek.

ered, spawned rainbows are closer to their spawning areas, thus more concentrated and easier to locate. (A guide friend fished there last May 15–20 and hooked over fifty fish a day.)

Water conditions. Should be recovering from low-flow cycle, providing optimum cover for fish and ideal float-boat conditions.

Suggested follow-up. Phone Joe Doaks Guide Service to assure ideal water conditions and success before departure.

Alternate areas to fish same trip. Rattlesnake Fork.

Tommy Stouffer was the author's casting mentor.

Bud Lilly fishing a favorite run on the Firehole.

Maps to take along. St. Peter National Forest, Indian Reservation.

Flies and tackle. Yellow and white Marabou Muddlers (sizes 8 through 4), San Juan Worm (sizes 8 & 6). Many caddis hatch there in May, so don't forget standard dries and nymphs. Fast, extra-fast, and intermediate sink-tip lines. Intermediate, fast- and extra-fast-sinking full sinking lines. Floating lines. Strike-indicators. Tippet sizes: 4X, 5X, 6X, two coils of each.

Tactics to remember. Look for 'bows near gravel and weed; for browns in shade. Best fishing for 'bows may occur in midday, after water warms and gets their "juices" flowing. Watch for 'bows and browns chasing baitfish tight against the shore and in the shallows after the sun is off the water. Remember to change to heavier tippet then. Don't lift the San Juan Worm from the water too soon. Sometimes they chase it right to the boat or bank.

"This process of planning sounds okay for long, expensive trips where you can justify avoiding a miscue by being extra careful," you say, "but what about that unplanned overnight jaunt to those streams down the valley? Heck, it's only a two-hour drive! Hardly sounds worth the effort."

My answer to that is, to be sure, it's only two hours down and two hours back with ten or twelve hours to fly fish. That's a total of sixteen or so well-deserved hours of recreation for me. Now, if I drive for two hours and find lousy fishing, then drive two hours back, I have wasted a fourth of the time that was available for me to fish. I've also wasted the cost of the trip. Why chance it when a quick phone call or two can ensure that you're heading for productive rainbow water at the outset?

Staying on Top of the Action

Knowing *where* to go fishing is genuinely helpful when you know precisely which areas of the lake or stream have recently produced good fly fishing and which hatches or forage fish movements happen to be occuring at that moment. If you're seeking steelheads, locating river runs is essential. To do this accurately, what are needed are contacts living close to the water whom one can phone and obtain accurate, timely information.

What staying on top of the action involves is establishing a network of reliable sources of information concerning the waters you intend to fish. Over the years, I've kept a file containing the names and phone numbers of individuals who can be counted on to lend a hand in accurately assessing the fishing in numerous lakes and streams close to and far from home. Keeping the file up-to-date is my secret of getting to know when, where, and how to fish a stream or lake *effectively* when I'm unable to be there throughout the season.

3

Finding Feeding Zones in Lakes and Streams

It had been a frustrating trip. My father and I had gone fishless for two days at the remote little lake in the British Columbia highlands. Our visit was timed to coincide with the hatching of thumb-joint-long caddis, known locally as "traveling sedges." But unseasonably cold, rainy weather seemed to have delayed their emergence. Using fast-sinking fly lines and Carey Special wet flies suggesting pupating caddis, we were unable to hook a fish.

On the third morning, we began by mooch-trolling leechlike streamer flies through a relatively shallow bay at the downwind end of the lake. There the bottom was heavily littered with debris drifted by wave-action. I had spotted some leeches in the extreme shallows and had decided to try the leechlike artificials in a last-ditch effort to catch some fish.

Just before lunch, a 12-inch Kamloops

rainbow tumbled to a brown Marabou Leech. As I removed the hook from the trout's mouth, a 2-inch leech, tumbled out. I killed that fish to check its stomach contents. Inside were a half-dozen leeches.

As I finished dressing the fish, I looked down into the water more closely. A veritable cloud of leeches undulated slowly by near the bottom. Since I had only one brown-colored leech, I rowed the 500 yards back to camp as fast as possible. While my dad whipped up lunch, I tied a half-dozen Marabou Leeches. And before too long we were once again mooching them through that downwind bay. The first fish to hit was a 12-incher, the second a 3-pounder.

This prompted us to drop anchor and cast, letting the flies sink to the bottom on the sinking lines before starting to strip them in. Several additional Kamloops tumbled for the ploy. Eventually,

"Mooch-trolling" on a little Canadian lake.

the leeches moved on, the Kamloops following them.

The strategy of mooch-trolling until a fish was hooked, then anchoring to cast, produced for the balance of the week. During that time we hooked and released a couple of hundred Kamloops, ranging from 10 inches to 7 pounds.

Although the sedge hatch failed to develop while we were at the lake, we still enjoyed some sort of fly fishing. We had located the *zone* in the lake where the fish were feeding, and we had also identified the *food* on which they were feeding at the moment.

Each lake or stream seems to have its own unique mix of habitats where rainbows habitually feed. The best fishing is usually found in areas that contain some sort of relatively immobile trout food, such as snails, shrimps, cress bugs, crayfish, or nymphs.

Other areas of a lake or stream, like the shallow bay in the Kamloops lake, attract rainbows only when food moves there, or becomes especially active or abundant. Good examples are downwind bays and coves on lakes (as just described), and oxbow bends in rivers. These are places where trout foods accumulate.

Rains produce such feeding zones by washing terrestrial or airborne insects into the water. Another sort of feeding zone develops when spawning steelheads or salmon run up a stream harboring resident rainbow trout. The rainbows tag along behind the migrating fish and feed on the eggs.

Feeding Zones in Lakes

Obviously, the best places in a lake or stream to flyfish for rainbows are the feeding zones. Let's call them *consistent* or *intermittent* feeding zones. The larger the water, the more difficult it is to find these zones. Perhaps the most difficult of all are large freshwater lakes and impoundments where the rainbow's feeding habits depend on the movement of such forage fishes as smelt, Kokanee salmon, alewives, ciscos, or threadfin shad. In other waters, the rainbow feeds on such mobile foods as mysis shrimps or leeches.

It's tricky to spot the movements of forage fish on a large lake, but once you do you'll have sensational fly fishing. Fish-eating rainbows often grow to extraordinary size. They also become highly aggressive in order to capture their elusive prey. Check inlets or outlets on large lakes. These are often the best places to find migrating forage fish.

When I lived in Washington state, I used to fish Kootenay Lake, in British Columbia, in September. I'd stay at the village of Balfour where the river exits the lake in an outflow several hundred yards wide. At that time of year, the trout were feeding on hordes of mysis shrimps, hatching blue dun mayflies, and schools of kokanee. The best fishing was at dawn and sunset. But it was worth the chilly discomfort: the rainbows averaged well over 3 pounds. The most effective tactic was to free-drift a dry Blue Dun, Irresistible, or Royal Trude straight downstream from my drifting boat. You didn't have to throw a long line, but your cast had to be straight and your float drag-free. If your presentation was right, you could hook a dozen or more hefty trout a day. I was saddened to hear from a friend that the fishing there has declined. Doubtless the major cause was the overly generous catch-limit allowed during the late '60s and early '70s.

On Irvine Lake, near my home in

Two large rainbows caught by the author and his friend, Tom Stouffer, from a large natural lake's outlet.

A magnificent stretch for migrating steelheads.

southern California, I've been able to track the movements of threadfin shad. I discovered their travel route past a certain point of land leading to the lake's inflow. Under high water conditions, the shad moved to and from the inflowing water past the point, which leads to a lightly weeded bay in which they sometimes feed. Mooch-trolling a shad-imitating streamer fly, such as the Whitlock's Shad, past that point has often yielded trout in excess of 4 pounds. Since Irvine Lake is normally fished with bait or trolled lures, my friends were surprised when I caught trout on streamer flies. Virtually no skill was needed to catch the trout. Finding the shad's travel routes was the key.

Feeding Zones in Streams

Broad, fast-flowing trout streams pose fascinating problems for an angler trying to locate rainbow trout. What makes this

On this Wisconsin trout stream, shade near a caddis-abundant riffle is used by the trout when they need protective cover.

difficult is that many of the prime rainbow feeding areas also may be used by other trouts.

Most species of stream trout tend to hold when *not* feeding in parts of the stream that are relatively protected. Rainbow trout like holding water with easy access to nearby food and within sight of currents that bring food downstream. Sometimes rainbows follow the food to its upstream source. When fishing caddis nymph flies upstream, I've often caught rainbows at my feet, or even downstream below me. Apparently, the fish move in behind me to feed on the caddis larvae I've dislodged from the stream bottom while wading.

Of course, trout often hold and feed in the same place. Small pools in tumbling canyon pocket water are one example. Trout remain in these pools behind boulders of various sizes. The larger trout usually prefer the larger pools with their greater abundance and variety of aquatic food. Another example is the small tunnel streams heavily overgrown by deciduous trees found from New England to Appalachia. Here, several rainbow feeding zones may be located within a few yards of each other. In the smaller tunnel streams, the feeding zones may be a matter of inches or feet from the trout's holding lies.

One such eastern stream I have fished is fairly typical. My favorite stretch consists of a long pool flowing into a calf-deep riffle at a bend, then into a knee-deep run flowing into a shaded pool downstream.

During the bright part of the day, the trout use the pools as a sort of "home base," concealing themselves in the shade of some fallen, partly submerged logs along the deeper shoreline. If there happens to be a caddis hatch in one of the riffles, the rainbows quickly move away from this cover and upstream to feed in the riffle, beating a hasty retreat to the pool once the hatch is over. In the evening, once again the trout "materialize" from the cover of the logs to feed.

The most significant thing to note here is the association between the upstream riffle and downstream pool. The fish don't hesitate to move from pool to riffle, even in broad daylight, when food is carried to them from that direction. Bear this in mind throughout this discussion.

In that same stream, another prime association exists where a culvert funnels the stream under a dirt road and into a deep, shaded pool. The current compressed by the culvert creates a mini-rapids fanning into the pool, creating both a current edge and slow-moving eddy off to one side. The current edge accumulates food drifting downstream, then slowly recirculates it around the eddy.

During an upstream hatch, the rainbows inhabiting that pool move quickly to cruise the current edge and eddy, then drift back into the shaded depths when the insects are gone.

Similar sets of associations for feeding rainbows occur on larger streams. In some, such as Armstrong Spring Creek in the Yellowstone valley in Montana, there may be a well-defined sequence of prime feeding waters in the riffles, weedy channels, runs, and deep pools.

When fishing these, it is helpful to visualize the pool as the trout's "home" territory. Its feeding patterns tend to flow *out* and *up* from that location. In these larger pools, the trout may be protected both by water depth and by rocky or weedy cover. Frequently such a pool will

Armstrong Spring Creek in Montana's Yellowstone valley.

harbor abundant forage fish, leeches, and aquatic insect life. In this sense, then, it can be considered to be one of the more consistent primes on the spring creek.

The moderately deep, rocky, channelized run directly upstream from the pool may become a prime when mayflies, stoneflies, and caddisflies are active there. The same may be true of the short riffle providing the transition between the pool and the run. Thus, as in the smaller tunnel stream, the *ascending* stretches of the spring creek may tend to relate to one another when trying to figure how to fish them.

On a much broader scale, sequences of rapids, riffles, runs and pools affect the behavior of the rainbows and other trouts in a larger stream or river. In these, the difference in targeting strategy may lie in determining how far upstream the rainbows home-basing in a certain pool may be willing to move when water conditions change, or when food becomes especially abundant in a certain stretch.

One particular section of the large river where we photographed some of the primes for this book comes to mind. Bud Lilly introduced it to me. And since it is a bit out of the way and requires a 4-wheel-drive vehicle or long hike to reach, I have little concern about your pinpointing its exact location and snaking out all the large trout before my next visit. However, because it happens to be one of Bud's favorite places to fish, in deference to him let's just call it the "Rattlesnake Fork" of the "Big Grizzly River."

There are two pools in this half-mile long reach of river. But the one I suspect serves as home-base for most of the rainbows lies at the lower end. It is fed by a short, powerful rapids, which flows into a deep, rocky run which tapers off into the pool.

Above the rapids, the river is divided by a gravelly island. On the pasture side, this forms a quarter-mile-long side channel. This is fed at the upper end by a short riffle emanating from the river's main channel. Halfway down the island, another short riffle cuts across the island, flowing into a deeper run of moderate current at the low end of the side channel.

Overall, this half-mile of river harbors an excellent population of rainbows, some large brown trout, a school of 12- to 18-inch cutthroats and a host of whitefish.

If one is seeking mainly rainbows, the stretch fishes best under normal to moderately high-water conditions. This is due to the greater turbulence and resulting higher oxygen level than existing in the side channel. In spring and summer, the side channel and the long eddy

Side-channels leading off from the main stem of large rivers sometimes prove to be rainbow trout bonanzas.

associated with the rapids-run-pool sequence below, hold an abundance of 14- to 16-inch rainbows, along with some larger fish.

Below the rapids, deep pockets formed by mid-river boulders at the edge of the heaviest current attract some hellaciously large rainbows. Bud proved this to me by hooking a heavy rainbow there that broke his eight-pound-test tippet.

The side channel upstream is more seasonally complex. It is more an intermittent prime for rainbows. The week prior to my arrival, the water had been running a foot or two higher. Bud had caught numerous rainbows using size 6 White Marabou Muddlers. When I arrived, the water had dropped. Then, the lower rapids, run, eddy, and pool harbored most of the rainbows in the bright part of the day.

The side channel was used mainly by browns, cutthroats, and whitefish until shadow hit the water in late afternoon. But as half-light approached, both rainbows and browns moved up into the channel's run, chasing minnows tight against the shoreline below the second island riffle.

The upper part of the channel was devoid of trout during the day, occupied mainly by a couple of large, solitary browns at dusk.

The rainbows pushing minnows against the island shore were approachable, but only from the island. Downstream, the rapids-run-pool complex seemed devoid of decent-sized trout in the evening hours.

Other large rivers, such as the Madison, offer long reaches of water posing a different sort of problem—water offering few apparent variations in texture and character. Viewed from afar, these may look more difficult to target than streams having clearly defined current sequences. But they are not, really.

Take the miles of the Madison River flowing in a continuous riffle above and below the MacAtee Bridge. This is a stretch I have fished off and on since the 1950s. There, with the exceptions of deeper-flowing runs and boulder-created deep pockets, rainbow trout hold sway.

Unlike the stretch of the "Rattlesnake Branch," just described, a panoramic viewing of the stream reveals little to indicate where to find feeding trout. It needs to be examined from streamside for that.

Once one does that when a hatch is in progress, it becomes quickly apparent that the heaviest feeding takes place where the riffles "flatten," slow a bit, and become deeper.

Because this reach of the Madison has few pools, the slower-moving stretches of riffles seem to be used by the trout for home-basing. Slack water created by huge boulders also plays a similar role. Movements of rainbows from these locations to shore waters and elsewhere appear mainly to stem from hatching aquatic insects and from terrestrials being washed or blown into the water.

When I have fished there in the late spring, and my trip has coincided with the hatching of the large stoneflies (Pteronarcys californicus), trout movement gravitates towards the shore waters. For then, the stoneflies are crawling onto the shore rocks to hatch, clambering about shoreline brush, ovipositing in the river and being washed along on the current in large numbers.

While the stoneflies are hatching, the waters closest to shore seem to attract

flat spot

Portions of riffles flatten out and slow enough to attract rainbows as a sort of home-base. This one is near the angler standing on the mid-stream island in the Madison River.

the largest numbers of rainbows. That is not to say some fish do not feed on stoneflies washed along by currents further out into the river. For they do. But the greater concentration of *feeding* fish appears to be nearer shore.

Brown trout inhabiting that stretch also gorge on the stoneflies, but their movements into the shore waters appear to be more closely associated with late-evening hours, than during midday, when the rainbows are most active. The larger browns also tend to hold to deeper-flowing stretches.

These Madison River riffles also harbor several varieties of caddisflies. Some of these hatches occur prior to the

stonefly bonanza and concurrent runoff period; others, intermittently throughout the summer and fall. And when the stoneflies aren't about, the caddisfly *activity* tends to strongly affect the rainbows' behavior.

Thundershowers washing beetles and ants into the streams, and strong winds from mid-morning through the afternoon plunking grasshoppers into the flow create other intermittant primes. At times, the trout virtually climb out onto the bank to avail themselves of the near-shore feeding opportunities.

But when the wind is not blowing hard, and when no caddis or mayfly hatches are occuring, the concentrations

A stretch of the Madison River, where the riffle flattens and slows. Most of the rainbows were gathered at the distinct current edge.

of rainbows seem to be mainly where the riffles drop and slow a bit, creating runs of relatively moderate current. Where some of these slower-moving stretches occur, bushes overhanging the bank also may be found, providing an ideal situation for trout to move to feed on beetles that fall off their branches into the water. The trout under these brushy overhangs can be in a highly aggressive mood at dawn.

Further downstream, the entire character of the Madison River changes after tumbling through Bear Trap canyon. Here, it is slower moving overall, consist-

ing mainly of riffles, runs, pools, and undercut banks. Here, brown trout hold more sway. And you'll find them holding tight up against the undercuts, under bushes, and in the deeper, slow-moving runs and pools.

Both the browns and the rainbows utilize the gravelly, channelized stretches for spawning at the appropriate seasons; the browns in the fall, the 'bows in the spring. At other times of year, the rainbows tend to frequent faster currents than the browns, provided there is adequate rock to break the current and afford protective cover. The feeding

Following thundershowers, rainbows work close to an overhanging shoreline to feed on washed-in terrestrials, like ants and beetles.

primes in this stretch also seem to be heavily influenced by the presence of crayfish and forage fishes.

Timing Intermittent Stream Primes

As one can readily understand after considering these select stream types, large and small, feeding primes are the result of the character of the trout habitat and seasonal food availability within it. The competition between rainbow trout and other species, or lack of it, also affects their locations. But what tends to shine through is that what applies to locations of primes on small-sized streams also is likely to apply to large rivers, except on a much grander scale.

One of the surest ways to be at the right place at the right time on intermittent primes is to understand when the fish move *through* them to migrate, or move *to* them to feed. Each stream seems to have its own unique timetable for the trout movements.

Getting a handle on the timing for the little tunnel stream or meadow spring creek certainly is much easier than on a large river. On the small-sized streams, a day on the water from sun-up to last-light normally provides a good feeling for feeding patterns at that particular time of year. Several days of observation may be needed to accomplish the same thing on the large freestone trout stream.

One reason for this, of course, is that the small stream may not afford the trout the varied diet more likely to exist in the large river.

There are several ways to go about tuning in on the intermittent primes on large-sized streams. Personal observation is perhaps the most reliable, though most time-consuming way to do it. However, if one is a well-networked fly fisher, past experiences on the water coupled with information gleaned from local anglers may be all that is necessary, even when fishing a stream with which one may be totally unfamiliar. The more time one spends on the water, the easier this process becomes, due to behavioral similarities of rainbows one may have encountered elsewhere.

The approach for the beginner or less-experienced fly fisher by necessity needs to be more academic. This angler may not be aware that springtime hatches and ovipositing may occur practically anytime, day or night; or, that summertime trout feeding tends to occur mainly early and late in the day; or, that fall and winter feeding activity mainly takes place from late in the morning through early evening. And he or she is most unlikely to be aware of any specific local hatches that may occur seasonally, without first having consulted with some local authority.

Take the late fall fly fishing on one of my favorite streams as an example. It is characteristic of the need for *very specific* information.

This particular stream is a large spring creek from which hatches of both Baetis and Callibaetis mayflies tend to come off, starting about one o'clock in the afternoon in the fall. Sometimes the hatches continue until it's too dark to see to cast.

Knowing that the tiny, size 18 and 16 mayflies also frequent relatively slow-moving, weedy stretches, allows me not only to isolate times to fish, but precise types of water where hatches are likely to occur. It also permits me to take full

Deep, rocky, weedy pools like this are often consistent rainbow trout primes.

advantage of other fly fishing opportunities nearby.

In this instance, I will fish large streamer flies for browns and rainbows in a larger, nearby freestone stream from first-light to 11:00 A.M. Then, I'll take a decent lunch break and drive to my pet spring creek in time to meet the afternoon rise.

The net result of timing one's fishing this precisely is that the best possible use of time on the water is made. The bottom line is a shortening of the intervals between strikes. Whether the timed fishing is focused on a gravelly shoal, a riffle, or on a slow-moving run or pool, the *accuracy* of the timing substantially contributes to the degree of success. And

that simply boils down to having more fun.

Timing the Consistent Stream Primes

Timing fly fishing to the consistent stream primes holding aggressive rainbow trout is fairly easy, because the variety of food organisms there tends to be greater, the fish less selective.

Some of the better consistent rainbow feeding locations include the confluences of feeder-springs with pools, the confluences of the stream with another stream or river, and slow-moving pools and runs with both boulder and weed cover. Channelized reaches also rank high.

There are at least eight good potential lies for rainbows in this canyon water. Can you identify them?

To a certain extent, timing fly fishing to rainbows inhabiting these locations depends less on insect hatching or mating activities than in other reaches of the stream. Having an extraordinary abundance so nearby seems to keep the rainbows more in the mood to feed when hatches or spinnerfalls are not underway. Thus, these sorts of locations are more than likely to produce some fish whenever one chances upon them.

Very deep, slow-moving, rocky-bottomed streams also are likely to provide consistent fly fishing for rainbow trout throughout the day, provided they harbor leeches or forage fish. And in some ways, the fishing of them more resembles that in lakes than in the fast-moving streams. Deep-flowing pools, backwaters, and eddies in large spring creeks bear similar characteristics. For it is in these slowest-moving parts of such streams that both the leeches and forage fishes tend to gather.

Obviously, one strategy for fishing the consistently productive reaches of a river is simply to "camp" there and persistently "dredge" the depths with leech or streamer flies, using sinking lines. It's one of the more important tactics when winter steelheading. But applied to spring, summer, and fall fishing for resident rainbows, it may result in bypassing intermittent waters capable of producing fantastic moments of action.

For that reason, my own strategy tends to focus on consistent primes mainly when no feeding activity is going on elsewhere. This results in a more interesting variety of fly fishing opportunities throughout the day without sacrificing the intermittent "highs" of trout feeding on other parts of the stream. The more familiar one becomes with a given stream, the more effective the strategy tends to be.

Characteristics of Stillwater Primes

Lake primes are often less distinct than those occurring in streams. As with streams and rivers, the size of the lake or pond tends to affect the ease with which the better rainbow feeding areas are targeted. As in streams, lake primes may be either of a consistent or intermittent nature. However, in viewing them, one needs to be mindful that practical limitations of *depth* affect one's ability to fish them at all.

Depth greater than thirty or forty feet essentially eliminates all but the shallower portions of large, deep lakes from fly fishing. Even lead-core shooting-taper lines, cast distances in excess of 100 feet, will not permit the effective probing of depths exceeding forty feet.

Knowing that one's fishing is restricted to the relatively thin upper portion of such a lake more or less automatically draws the fly fisher's attention towards whatever depths may be fishable within the limitations imposed by the tackle. This, in turn, may draw one's attention away from deeper areas where intermittent feeding primes do occur. For this reason, seeking smaller, shallower rainbow trout lakes tends to be the more consistently effective overall strategy. In these, the recognizable opportunities are more quickly read without the need for sophisticated, electronic fish-locating equipment.

Identifying Consistent Lake Primes

Perhaps the easiest way to isolate consistently productive areas of the rainbow

This lake is less than forty acres, yet it contains trout up to two pounds.

trout lake to fish is to look not so much for actively feeding trout—though that never should be ignored—but for habitats which usually harbor trout foods. Certain of the most common trout food organisms are more or less "bound" to specific sorts of habitats. The flyfishable sorts of habitats are quite easy to identify visually, provided one starts with a knowledge of the needs of the lake-inhabiting trout foods themselves.

Ideal lake-inhabiting foods for trout include dragonfly nymphs, damselfly nymphs, mayfly nymphs, caddis and Chironomid larvae and pupae, snails, freshwater shrimps, crayfish, leeches, trout and salmon alevins, and forage fishes. Each of these tends to relate to certain habitats within the lakes in which they are found.

Dragonfly and damselfly nymphs, and some mayfly nymphs, oftentimes will be found associated with the weedy environments fostering production of their food organisms. The same is true of shrimps and snails.

Crayfish, on the other hand, hibernate through the winter months in soft-bank burrows, emerging from these in the spring and quickly migrating to rocky areas, in which they find concealment during the bright parts of the day. Much of the feeding on crayfish appears to be done mainly after dark, or at the least, at depths where light penetration is relatively poor.

Chironomid larvae and certain mayfly nymphs are silt-burrowers. Other mayfly nymphs may be found in rocky, gravelly, or weedy parts of the lake. Lake-inhabiting caddis frequently are found on detritis bottoms. The larvae will construct cocoons resembling "hedge-hogs" or tubes from the bits and pieces of plants and sticks found on the littered lake bottom.

In the more eminently flyfishable lakes and ponds, which tend to be relatively shallow overall, most of the rainbow's food will be found associated with the relatively shallow areas which biologists refer to as the "food shelf." Here, light penetration promotes weed growth and photosynthesis, which supplies oxygen to the water in sunlit conditions.

And it is on the food shelf "zone" of the lake where *feeding* rainbows are most likely to be found within reach of flyfishing tactics, and where the trout are most likely to be aggressive. This food-shelf lake zone, then, can be thought of by the fly fisher as the lake's *most consistent* prime.

Although the lake's surface presents numerous intermittently ideal flyfishing opportunities, both on emerging and

This angler has hooked a 14-inch rainbow in a weedy channel.

hatching aquatic insects and fallen terrestrials, it is more like the shore waters of the stream. The flurries of trout feeding occur mainly when insects move there to hatch, adult insects are fallen or ovipositing, or forage fish are concentrated to feed on near-surface plankton.

Several seasonal implications come to mind when considering the rainbow's feeding patterns on a lake's food shelf. For, although we may be aware that the shelf harbors relatively abundant trout food throughout much of the calendar year, the most aggressive feeding there by the trout occurs when water temperatures have their "juices" going strong. Happily, that is normally when the food organisms are also most active.

At lower elevations, say up to about 2500 feet, this occurs both in the spring and fall months, when water temperatures range between 50 and 65 degrees F. Elsewhere, it will occur whenever the aquatic springtime or fall conditions come about.

Later in the season, unacceptable pH values in the food shelf waters, due to "blooming" plankton, may cause the trout to move *from* them whenever such conditions occur.

Additional conditions tend to affect the trouts' willingness to remain in the food-shelf portions of the lake. These are both structurally and water-quality related. They include submerged creek channels, underwater depressions and humps, underwater-sourced springs, seasonal cycles of pondweed growth, and water clarity.

Like the stream, the lake undergoes almost constant changes in its environments that affect flyfishing from moment to moment. Were it not undergoing these changes, we would

undoubtedly catch a lot more trout from it than we do.

For example, springs emanating from beneath the lake bottom tend to attract rainbows when water temperatures throughout adjacent shallow areas may be uncomfortably warm. This may prompt the trout to remain there a good deal further into the summer than one might expect in other parts of the lake of similar depth. Creeks and streams inletting the lake may provide a similar summertime attraction to the trout.

In other situations, the kinds of pondweeds "knocked down" by winter ice-over may offer the trout a feeding opportunity well after ice-out and "overturn" in the spring.

And in still others, blooms of plankton may so affect the pH of the food shelf waters, and the water clarity, that the trout move to clearer, more comfortable waters beneath the blooms. The blooming algae rarely extend down into the lake at depths greater than ten feet. This may guide the angler to exploring deeper portions of the food shelf lying beneath the bloom, which at the surface may appear as unfishable as pea soup.

Identifying Intermittent Lake Primes

Lake areas to which rainbow trout *move* to feed sporadically may exist within or outside of the food shelf. The most easily recognized of these include the water's surface film; inlet and outlet streams; underwater structures attractive to forage fishes; timber-bordered creek channels; and thermal, pH, clarity, and depth breaklines.

Inflowing and outflowing streams are attractive to rainbows, because of the periodic appearance there of spawning or feeding forage fishes and other food organisms concentrated there by current. An area adjacent to an inlet can be looked upon very much like a pool in a trout stream, into which are flowing riffles or rapids. The moving current provides intermittent influxes of food, which are carried into the lake. Both the rainbow trout, other trouts, bass, pike, and forage fishes may be attracted—the forage fish being the main attraction to the trout and other predatory game fish.

In the event the inlet stream is adjacent to rocky structures, then the attraction to the trout may be even greater. For this type of lake bottom structures provides a clearly defined "travel route" to and from the inlet for both the trout and the forage fish to instinctively follow. Extensive food-shelf weed cover nearby may also cause numerous trout to "take up residence" in the general area of the inlet or outlet.

But outlet streams are less predictable than inlets. Like the outlet at Balfour, British Columbia, described earlier, the trout's presence may depend entirely on the periodic appearance of certain food organisms. When viewing outlets for flyfishing opportunities, the initial look-see should be a panoramic one, encompassing distance along the lake shores adjacent to them. The character of those waters sometimes reveals the attraction to trout of the outlet proper.

Of the two, inlets tend to provide more *predictable* flyfishing opportunities, if not more consistent ones.

One of the more interesting of these in the entire western United States exists where the Owens River pours into Crowley Lake, in the eastern Sierras of California.

Each October, hordes of immature Sacramento Perch appear in the weedy shallows on the sunny inlet side of the lake. Sacramento Perch are the only members of the sunfish family actually native to waters west of the Rocky Mountains.

The presence of the immature perch roughly coincides with the movement of the lake's mature brown trout towards the lake's inlet for spawning purposes. Simultaneously, the Crowley Lake rainbows, which like the browns tend to be of substantial size, go on their fall feeding binge.

Brown trout moving into the vicinity of the inlet sometimes linger to gorge on the perch, as brown trout often do in river pools during their spawning runs. Both the browns and rainbows forage up and down the shoreline on perch.

With such a large proportion of the lake's mature trout population concentrating against a couple of miles of shoreline, what follows often turns out to be a flyrodder's mother lode. Streamer flies suggesting the small perch, such as the Olive Matuka streamer, presented towards shore from a float tube or small boat, provoke plenty of smashing attacks by the fish. The phenomenon lasts for several weeks.

Two main types of rainbow trout forage inhabit rocky lake structures. These are the crayfish and the forage fish. If the bottom structure of the lake forms some sort of "reef system," it often constitutes a reliable source of minnows and forage species for the trout to feed upon. The young of any trout species are as seasonally attractive to the 'bows as the forage fishes.

If the rocks mainly attract crayfish, then the rainbows may move there only

Old creek channels bordered by timber in impoundments are among the more consistent producers of outstanding rainbow trout fly fishing.

during those times of year when the crayfish are clambering about the rocks. The prime feeding time for trout working on crayfish usually occurs well after dark when the crayfish are most active.

Artificially constructed lakes and impoundments having an abundance of downed and standing timber in the water are among the more consistent producers of outstanding rainbow fly fishing. Oftentimes, the trout's food supply in these lakes consists of abundant

caddis or forage fish. Where the timber is down and branches form cover breaking the rainbow's silhouette, the trout tend to use the cover to ambush passing schools of baitfish.

The channels between the stands of timber, which often conceal long-submerged creek channels, can be looked upon as places where the rainbows may be found cruising in search of food. In stiff breezes, particularly if the channel happens to be only a few feet deep, an almost stream-like condition tends to occur. Wind-induced current causes the rainbows to hold "on station" and take in food morsels drifting to them. When this happens, perhaps the most effective tactic is to anchor your boat or float tube and cast up-wind, retrieving the nymph or streamer fly in a downstream direction in the wind-pushed current.

As indicated earlier, the various kinds of breaklines occurring in lakes also promote intermittent flurries of feeding by rainbows. The feeding zone under blooming algae already has been described. Another sort of clarity breakline results from snow runoff bringing turbid water into the lake through inlet streams or along soft-banked shorelines. Scuba divers indicate that trout and other game fish tend to lurk in the off-color water to conceal themselves from forage fishes cruising in the clear water.

Stained, tea-colored lake water creates a breakline of a different character, the upper few feet of the lake being the prime location in which to fish. Lakes of this kind are found across the breadth of the northern-tier states and southern reaches of some Canadian provinces.

In these "dark-water" lakes, one can think of the upper clarity layer as the portion of the lake containing trout, the lower layer containing little or no aquatic life. The reason this is true is that sunlight cannot penetrate deeply enough to promote weed growth at greater depths than a few feet. The fish-holding lake layer may extend only eight or ten feet below the surface, greatly simplifying the search for the trout.

Relatively sudden changes in depth also constitute breaklines attracting rainbows. As youngsters we knew these as "drop-offs." Some of the drop-offs most attractive to rainbows are the sides of long underwater points of land, the drop-offs leading from the food shelf to deep water. The edges of old creek channels on impoundments also form attractive breaklines for the trout. So do underwater humps.

In most of these situations, and when the water in the shallows is uncomfortably warm, the rainbows often retreat to the depths when not actually feeding. In this sense, the deep water off the breakline constitutes *depth cover* for the trout. In lakes, depth is often used by the trout as shade cover might be in a stream lacking deep pools for concealment.

When viewing these depth breaklines as feeding areas, it helps to understand they frequently serve as travel-routes leading to the shallower food shelf, not only for trout but also for bass and other species of fish. When weeds are present along the depth breakline, it also may serve as a haven for forage fish and immature game fish. The weeds also are likely to harbor various kinds of aquatic insects. As a result, the lake drop-offs can be viewed as relatively consistent trout primes in warm weather and during the middle of the day when the trout tend to retreat to them to escape rising pH or water temperature in the shallows.

Identifying thermal and pH breaklines requires the use of suitable electronic gear. My suggestion is to seriously consider purchasing this gear if you habitually fish deep lakes and impoundments. Over the long haul, the cost of the equipment may be well worth it—it has been for me fishing the big Southwestern impoundments for rainbows, largemouth bass, smallmouth bass, striped bass, and crappies.

The pH meter used in conjunction

with a good paper-graph sonar is invaluable in locating those *zones* of the impoundments where the fish tend to be aggressive and which can be reached with sinking fly lines. They save one a great deal of fruitless trial-and-error fishing.

Steelhead Holding Primes

It was late November. The air temperature was 40 degrees F. And my lightly built companion shuddered visibly as the chill from the water cut through his waders. We were fishing the lower, slower-moving reach of the Outhouse Run on Idaho's Clearwater River. Because of the cool water, we figured that the lower end of the stretch, where it slowed noticeably from the moderate rapids upstream might hold a fish or two.

My friend Al Cunningham had strung his rod back at camp. I was almost finished stringing mine when I heard an ex-

This slow-moving stretch of water at the confluence of two steelhead rivers is used by migrating summer-runs to hold over the winter months.

cited "Oh, boy!" I looked up to see his rod tip throbbing threateningly up and down, indicative of a big steelhead shaking its head before fully reacting to the hook-set. The fish had hit a size 2 green-butted Skunk as it swung deeply past a huge, submerged boulder in current flowing into the pool's edge-water.

He was fishing with a Hi-D shooting taper. Loose coils of 30-pound-test monofilament shooting-line still lay on the water. I started to shout to him that he should reel in that slack line before the fish ran. But I was too late. The fish had turned and lunged into faster-moving current like a fullback heading for "three yards and a pile of dust." The mono lashed through the fly rod guides like the loose end of a broken high-voltage line.

Suddenly, Al's rod was yanked savagely into the water, almost from his blue-knuckled grasp. He was almost pulled from his balance on the slippery river bottom. Then, there was a snapping "twang" that left him standing there shaken and disappointed. The shooting taper line followed the great steelhead into the greenish-black depths of the river. A coil of the shooting-line had half-hitched one of the large buttons at his jacket sleeve cuff. He hadn't seen it happen until the line came taut.

Fifty yards out into the river the huge fish rolled heavily to the surface, still trailing the line. From the breadth of the tail, one could easily surmise it was a steelhead in the 20-pound class.

While Al trudged back to the truck to extract another shooting taper from his kit, I stepped into the water and cast to the same spot. The steelhead that grabbed the fly, almost at the instant I started a stripping recovery, weighed between 12 and 15 pounds.

Transitions in current speed frequently help identify steelhead holding lies. In this case, the edge between different currents was a subtle one. You could scarcely discern it from the rest of the pool. But experiences of the previous fifteen years had proven that this one, located well below where the rapids slowed and formed a deep, run-like pool, often held steelheads when the water temperature dropped below 55 degrees F. This day, it ranged in the upper 40s.

When the water is in the warmer range more associated with upstream movement by summer-run steelheads, transitions in current also help identify lies where the fish hold to rest. Many of these are located relatively close to the tops of rapids. Often they will range between three and eight feet in depth. Most often they occur in a stretch having circuitous channels cut through ledgerock, or where there are large boulders.

Other holding waters may appear to be rocky runs of moderate depth where one would expect to find steelhead "moving through," rather than holding. The general character of the river influences this a good deal, in my opinion.

On some of the steelhead streams I've fished in Michigan, and some of the short western coastal rivers experiencing mainly winter runs of steelheads, the river may move only a few miles through relatively gentle pools and runs before shallowing to the gravelly bottoms where the steelheads prefer to spawn. In these, the holding stretches may only consist of a few pools, which in the case of winter-run fish may be used for only

Typical cold-water holding stretch on a large, western steelhead river.

a brief time before they hustle into the spawning act.

Steelhead Traveling Primes

Current speed transitions play a like role in helping to identify steelhead travel routes. These travel routes tend to be the exact same ones used by the fish for centuries past, changing only when significant changes occur in the river bottom.

Most of the travel routes lead *through* places in the river where the fish also hold when not moving upstream. At times, both traveling and holding fish may be taken from these.

Other travel routes are more clearly defined as places where *only* moving fish are caught. These usually lack adequate rock cover for holding in faster currents. Good examples include the long, rocky runs between sets of riffles, and where the main current flow is funneled along a deeper cut along a rocky shoreline. In these latter runs, the steelheads almost invariably will be "hit" where the current seam separates the main thrust of the flow from slower waters to the side.

In most instances, "rock" is a common link to identifying both travel routes and holding waters. I suspect this is true because well-anchored rock ledges and boulders constitute the most stable form of river bottom. They're the least likely parts of the river to be altered by ice-out, runoff, or powerful flooding conditions.

Some of the better traveling waters exist at the foot of rapids, where the rapids churn over rocks into the pool. The deeper, slower-moving current edges seem to be more associated with holding fish, based on my experience. This is particularly true of where the current tongue fans out into the pool over a boulder-strewn river bottom. This sort of location seems to be where steelhead pods "stack up" just prior to an early morning dash through the rapids immediately upstream.

Not infrequently, traveling steelheads indicate their presence by knifing through the surface of the water. Although this may tend to heighten one's anticipation initially, at times it may prove disappointing. For it has been my experience that "rolling" steelheads, particularly winter-run fish, often show little interest in the fly.

At other times, rolling steelheads do come to the fly with gusto. This occurred during extremely low water conditions along the Snake River.

On this occasion, steelheads had been holding for several weeks in downstream pools. This was known to be true due to miniature radio transmitters attached to some of the steelheads.

A "classic" stretch of steelhead traveling water on a coastal river.

The author observed this magnificent 15-pound, 8-ounce male summer-run steelhead roll prior to hooking it on a size 2 Green-Butted Skunk bucktail.

When viewing a stretch of river for current edges, it helps to get well above the streambank.

seam

One evening the weather conditions changed ever so slightly. Although no detectable rise in water appeared to be taking place, a few fish started moving up through the long run and riffles immediately below the confluence of the Grand Ronde River with the Snake. Numerous fish were rolling.

The few fly fishermen on the river at that half-hour "moment" in the early evening practically all hooked at least one fish. When the periodic rolling of fish ceased, so did the hits. That pod of fish had obviously moved past us and into the mouth of the Grand Ronde. An angler fly fishing there when the action in the downstream run ceased hooked three fish in rapid succession.

As in targeting resident rainbows in streams, sometimes it is helpful to take a panoramic view of the steelhead river while trying to identify travel routes. I like to get some distance, several hundred yards, higher than the stream bank to do this. This higher viewpoint often reveals current edges which cannot easily be identified from streamside.

Sometimes an even more encompassing view of the stream, taken from a quarter mile or more away from the water will provide the best feel for where the main current flows more to one side of the river than the other. Several viewpoints may be required to determine this accurately.

The tyro steelhead fly fisher should be cautioned that even this strategy may not provide an absolute indication of where the travel route exists. But on an unfamiliar stretch, it may provide a more accurate guess than that taken from the water's edge.

Other strategic steps are involved in zeroing-in on likely lake and stream locations to meet rainbows and steelheads. When to fish certainly is one of the more important of these considerations, as the reader will discover in the next chapter.

4
When to Fish for Rainbows

Two of the fastest hours of flyfishing for rainbows I ever had occurred during a spring deluge. My friend Tom Stouffer and I had anchored over a weedy portion of the lake. The day was bright and sunny. The rainbows were biting. We were so preoccupied with hooking and releasing them on Dandy Green Nymphs we failed to notice the squall bearing down on us until it was too late.

The blast of rain hit full force, drawing the anchor ropes taut, drenching us to the skin before we could pull on rain suits. We were fishing so close to the boat-launch area that we hadn't bothered to mount the outboard motor and had rowed out to the weed bed a couple of hundred yards away. The rain was so heavy you couldn't see the shoreline. Visibility was limited to 20 feet at the most. Since there was no lightning, we

decided to stick it out until the rain stopped rather than risk getting lost. We scrambled into rain gear, sipped hot coffee, and decided to keep on fishing. I side-armed 20 feet of line and leader downwind, letting the size 4 nymph trail and work in the wind-driven surface current. The fly was scarcely in the water when a 3-pound rainbow jumped on it and surged downwards towards the weeds. As I turned that fish, Tom's fly rod folded into a deep parabola. His fish weighed more than mine, and came close to jumping into the boat before he got it under control.

Although most of the fish we hooked later ran between 11 inches and a couple of pounds, the action was practically nonstop until the rain stopped two hours later. We each had hooked nearly 100 trout. I've only had a half-dozen similar experiences in a lifetime of fly fishing. The rainbows simply went bananas while the rain was falling.

Why this occurred was fairly obvious. Before the rain started, there was an immense hatch of dragonflies and damselflies. The deluge dumped thousands of them into the lake, and the trout went into a feeding frenzy.

Because of experiences similar to this one, I've been intrigued by hackneyed old expressions such as: "The best time to go fishing is when you can!" If you will pardon the expression, quite a few hold water. This one applies to flyfishing for rainbow trout in all four seasons, for you can catch rainbows almost any time of the year. Nevertheless, it is possible to increase the *consistency* of your catches by careful timing. Certain aquatic seasons afford much better fly fishing than others, although peaks of good fishing occur in all of them.

Spring is one of the two prime seasons for flyfishing for rainbows. Two fishing peaks occur within it virtually everywhere throughout the rainbow's range. These are the spawning run and the feeding flurry that follows it.

The spawning run *concentrates* rainbows where they are especially vulnerable. Normally this will be in water which is relatively shallow over gravelly or rocky lake and stream bottoms. When presented a sunken fly having a touch of red color in it, the spawning rainbows quickly respond. Whether they do this to protect the nest or to feed is academic from the tactical viewpoint. Trout I have dressed during the spawning period have had some food in their digestive tracts. Others have attacked the fly so aggressively that nest-protection seemed

to be the most likely explanation. What's important to the fly fisher is that the trout's behavior is altogether predictable.

Strong arguments can be advanced with regard to the sportsmanship of fishing for rainbows when they're spawning. Whether or not you fish for them at this time is a matter of your personal ethics. One factor to consider is whether it will have a detrimental effect on the rainbow population of the lake or stream.

The second peak occurring during the spring starts soon after the rainbows depart their spawning redds. Water temperatures may have warmed sufficiently to promote aquatic insect movement and hatching activity. And as this develops, the spring feeding binge of the trout gets underway.

Although this grand flyfishing opportunity for lake rainbows normally occurs several weeks after ice-out and water turnover, on streams it may begin well before the run-off of melting snow waters. Caddisflies, in particular, may hatch prolifically prior to the run-off.

Some anglers aren't aware that some early-season fringe hatches provide fabulous fishing. Oftentimes, they will schedule trips to streams to meet major hatches taking place at the same time of year as the snow run-off. Although hatches may be massive, the actual quality of the fly fishing may be inferior to that occurring prior to the run-off.

The summer months are the ideal ones for rainbow fly fishing at higher elevations. The spawn and spring gorge offer flyfishing opportunities paralleling those found in lowland waters a month or two earlier. Early summer is "spring" to the rainbows finning in high alpine lakes and streams. The aquatic summer

In this lake high in Washington state's Cascade Range, spring-like aquatic conditions existed in mid-July.

The summer months constitute a prime flyfishing season at higher elevations on spring creeks like Silver Creek, Idaho. The author is pictured here.

for fish above 5000 feet elevation may not actually occur until late July or August, if ever.

True "aquatic" summer is characterized by relatively low water, periodic hatching of aquatic insects, the appearance of terrestrial insects, and less midday feeding by trout. At lowland lakes, summer often is the next to the poorest season for fly fishing for rainbows. At the high lakes in the Rockies, it frequently is the best, because conditions there represent aquatic springtime.

The second prime season for North American resident rainbow trout occurs in the fall. At high-altitude waters, this may be August or early September. Fall water conditions can be characterized as being low, clear, and cool. Insect hatching may be at its peak in the midday period. An abundance of summer-hatched forage fish and trout fry also may contribute to the rainbow's aggressiveness at this time of year. The fighting qualities of the trout are at their best, as well. They are fat and robust from spring and summer feeding, in top physical condition to offer flyrodders the thrill-

Fall steelheading at its best. A 12-pound female taken on a Fall Favorite.

ing battles for which the rainbow is most reknowned.

Indian summer ranks near the top of the list for the quality of its fall fishing. It follows close on the first frosts. Days are unbelievably mild, hazy, and sunny. The leaves turn intensely and the trout are active, willing.

Indian summer is when fly fishers delight to the realization that all football fanatics are not fly fishers. When pebble-skipping ten-year-olds, kayakers, canoeists, and river-tubers do not exist. When you can lie on the bank and nap after lunch and be assured of waking in time to meet some sort of rise. It is the season of intimacy with nature and trout.

You can flyfish for rainbows in winter, too. But it is not a prime season for doing so in the northern hemisphere. Perhaps the most favorable winter flyfishing conditions exist in tailwaters below dams and in spring creeks emanating from sources where the water temperatures remain constant throughout much of the year. These waters are likely to be warmer than nearby lakes and freestone streams, usually prompting some insect hatching.

Winter fly fishing in lakes tends to be a hit-and-miss proposition. When the lake is free of ice-cover, brief periods of feeding do occur. But the rainbows tend to be lethargic. They rarely come to the fly aggressively. And when they do, the great fighting qualities they exhibited during the spring, summer, and fall months are less evident.

When to Fish for Steelheads

Although West Coast runs of summer steelheads occur in fewer rivers and offer lower numbers of generally smaller fish than winter-runs, summer-run steelheads afford the prime flyfishing opportunities.

One reason is that the western winter season is fraught with great variations in water level and clarity. A river that might fish low one day, may turn into a turbid, surging torrent the next.

Due to winter rains and intermittent thaws, the fishing tends to be far less predictable than it is during the summer and fall.

There is a difference in the way winter-run and summer-run steelheads come to the fly, as well. Because they must hasten upstream and spawn so soon after entering fresh water, winter-run fish mature sexually at a more rapid rate than the summer-run steelheads. Actual spawning may commence within a few weeks after entering the river. If you don't meet the run before they've gone on the redds, they've lost much of their fighting ability.

Summer-run steelheads do not mature until the spring following their arrival in the river. As a result, they're charged with the zip and vitality needed to travel as far as several hundred miles inland and to sustain themselves for several months before spawning. When caught soon after entering the river, the summer-runs dazzle anglers with their speed, power, and determination.

Winter-run steelheads tend to hold fairly close to the river bottom and to move shorter distances to the fly than summer-run fish. It's often necessary to bounce the fly right along the river bottom to catch them. Heavily weighted flies and extra-fast-sinking lines may be needed to reach them in fast-flowing, heavily tinged currents. Greater persistence also may be needed, because they

This female rainbow, caught in late February, very obviously was into the spawning cycle. It was released by my friend Fenton Roskelley to fight far better on a much warmer day.

are not as predictably aggressive as summer-run fish. Fishless days are more common in winter-run fishing than in the summer.

Summer-run steelheads, in contrast, move extremely well to flies fished on or near the surface. "Dredging" for them with sinking lines is rarely necessary until water temperatures dip below 55 degrees F. Until the temperatures drop into the 40s and 30s, the summer-run's fighting qualities remain superb.

Because of the severity of the winters in the Great Lakes region, the best fly-fishing opportunities come before the onset of freezing weather and in the spring when the water temperatures have warmed. Although fish arriving in the fall come readily to flies, fish trickling in during the cold months are less responsive, like West Coast winter-runs. Fly fishing improves again in the spring—some of the best is in March and April, depending on the river. The fall fish respond well to both egg-type and western fly patterns; winter fish respond better to brighter, fluorescent ties. In clear water, more natural looking artificials may bring about strikes.

Prime Days of the Week

Any day of the week often is considered "prime time" by the frequent fly fisherman. Where rainbows are fished for mainly with bait, that frequently is *not* true.

It is often the practice of the bait fisherman to literally dump into the lake or stream whatever bait may be left following a day on the water. Their doing this didn't really affect my thinking about how the dumping practice might affect trout feeding patterns until one of my fishing pals casually noted that over the years he'd always seemed to have the best fly fishing on THURSDAYS. He also had determined that the three-day period following the weekend produced the poorest fly fishing.

Why?

Well, he had reasoned that the rainbows simply were so gorged after the weekend, that it took the trout three days to recover from the effects of eating what was dumped into the water. What my friend had said prompted me to seriously review my own fishing logs for a possible correlation. I also asked other flyfishing friends to do the same. All the logs checked indicated distinctly better fly fishing along towards the end of the week. The pattern was remarkably consistent.

Today, I instinctively head for flyfishing water late in the week. Over the years, this seems to have improved my consistency. The exception is fishing on waters where bait is not permitted. On those, the weekend tends to produce poorer results; the mid-week period, better results. This may be because there is lighter fishing then, disturbing the trout less. You may find that this little observation improves your own results when incorporated into a general trout fishing strategy. If so, all the better.

Prime Times of Day

I have touched here and there in other chapters on the subject of the time of day to fish for rainbows. The reason I have done so is that it is critical to accurate targeting. The time of day affects the temperature of the water, which affects aquatic and terrestrial insect activity, such as hatching and ovipositing.

The prime feeding times of trout relate mainly to the abundance, availability, and activity of their food organisms. But the rainbow's aggressiveness and relative lack of shyness generalizes the feeding behavior.

Numerous on-the-water experiences have proven to me that rainbow trout can be coaxed into taking a fly when no hatch is imminent or taking place. In this sense, the particular time of day one fly-fishes for rainbows may not be as important as it is when fishing for shade- and nocturnally-oriented brown trout. This constitutes one of the advantages enjoyed when fishing for the rainbows.

What about those occasions when the 'bows are feeding most actively on hatches? Is the time of day important then?

The answer, of course, is yes. But my experience has been that its importance is less specific than when brown trout fishing: The rainbow feeds over longer spans of time.

For example, if you're fly fishing a lake for rainbows in the springtime, and you start your fishing at dawn, you are very likely to catch some rainbows for a period of several hours prior to the water's warming a bit and prompting insect activity. Although the prime time of day may be between 9:30 A.M. and 2:00 P.M., there is a good chance you'll catch some fish both before and after the dragonflies and damselflies are actively moving about and hatching.

Take the freestone trout stream during the midsummer period. The water has probably dropped to a fairly low level. During the day, it's bright and sunny. And both the browns and the rainbows may have taken to some sort of protective cover. You know where the browns will be! In the shade of boulders, tucked back under the undercuts, deep in a shaded pool. If you say to yourself that the rainbows will be where the browns are hiding, you'll likely be wrong. Some of the 'bows will retreat to brown trout lies, to be sure. If the water is low, the amount of oxygen in the deeper, slower-moving river may not be as suitable to the rainbows as that in the riffles, or where a rapids churns oxygen into the water at the head of a pool.

Although the main insect hatches may occur on that stream early or late in the day—and most of the browns you'll catch will be taken then—your knowledge of how rainbows gravitate to well-oxygenated stretches may produce hookups throughout much of the day. At least, it may if you confidently work those waters with flies. Summer-run steelheads locate similarly at midday in low-water conditions throughout the summer and fall seasons.

The peak of the flyfishing action during the fall and winter periods tends to occur from sometime late in the morning to early in the afternoon. If a hatch occurs in that period, the prime feeding may begin an hour or so before the hatch, when the insect nymphs or pupae become active in the water. Yet, it may also extend well into the waning hours of daylight, well past the conclusion of the hatch.

In this general sense, then, it's fair to say that the rainbow is somewhat less time-selective than the brown trout. One is likely to find him exposed to flyfishing tactics far more often than browns.

Rainbow trout tend to be as ''broad-minded'' concerning which patterns of flies they'll respond to, as they are about the times of day when they'll bite. In Chapter 5, we'll discuss how you can turn this to your advantage.

5

A Commonsense Approach to Fly Selection

Any practical approach to fly selection tends to apply as much to other species of trout as it does to rainbow trout. The rainbow's adaptability to different food sources is reflected in its willingness to come to a variety of flies. They tend to be *less selective* than brown trout.

For many fly fishers, the simplified approach of some professional fishing guides may be the best one. When you fish only a few waters in a given region, few patterns may be needed to produce consistent results.

One of the best flyfishing guides I know often starts his clients fishing with a large nymph, a "big black one." If that doesn't work, he suggests the angler change to a "smaller gray one." That fly failing to produce, he hands the angler a "little olive one."

Another guide whom I respect totes

along mainly Royal Wulff and Royal Trude dries and wets, covering sizes from 18 through 2. And chances are, if you or I restricted our flies to those the two guides depend upon, and spent more effort achieving convincing presentations to the trout, we would probably catch more and larger fish than when drawing upon a more extensive fly selection.

The truth of this was brought to bear two years ago, when my friend Allan Rohrer and I were fishing a slow-moving irrigation ditch having spring creek-like qualities. I had started the day using a size 16 Zug Bug fished a couple of feet below a bright red strike indicator. I caught several trout fishing upstream with this rigging. Then, a nice rainbow grabbed the nymph and raced into the weeds, tearing the indicator from the tip-

Although the author is an accomplished fly tier, he also prefers simple flies, like this Dragonfly Nymph, for rainbow trout fishing. This one is varied in shades of olive, brown, or black to match regional color differences in naturals.

pet. Lacking another, I cut a short piece of poly-yarn and knotted it securely into a fresh tippet, dabbing the yarn-indicator with floatant to assure its floating high on the water.

Much to my surprise, three of the next five fish nailed the yarn strike indicator instead of the nymph!

Thinking this might indicate a hatch about to come off, I removed the yarn-indicator and replaced it with a size-14 Elk Hair Caddis. Rainbows often accept this pattern during hatches of both caddis and similarly-colored mayflies.

A pod of four rainbows was working where the current quickened over shallow gravel, then dropped into a pocket. The first fish hit the nymph. So did a second and a third trout. So much for my theory.

By this time, I was as puzzled as I was amused. So, for the fun of it, I retied a

Variations on the time-tested Royal Coachman fly pattern are among the deadliest for rainbow trout fishing, including the Royal Trude, Royal Wulff, and Royal Coachman Bucktail.

The Elk Hair Caddis is one of the most useful dry fly patterns in the rainbow trout fisherman's box. The trout go for it during caddis and some mayfly hatches.

poly-yarn indicator. On the next cast, whammo! A truly outsized rainbow belted the yarn instead of the nymph!

Fortunately for the fly merchants, all rainbow trout aren't quite that cooperative under all conditions. There are times when accurate representations of the naturals produce better results. This is frequently the case during mating flights of ants, hatches of Chironomids, and hatches of both Callibaetis and Baetis mayflies on the waters I tend to frequent.

Despite this periodic selectivity, even when rainbows show a preference for a particular color and size of insect, they'll often respond to quite different ties. Their selectivity "window" seems to have a more comprehensive "pane" than that of the brown trout.

Take what occurred on Silver Creek, Idaho, as an example. Awesome hatches of Trichorythodes mayflies were coming off.

When I arrived on the water in early afternoon with Lee Gomes and Tom Stouffer—long-time friends and angling companions—clouds of the tiny, white-winged naturals whirled like snow. The trout were feeding freely on the hatching duns. But nearby anglers were having trouble coaxing the trout to take their size 24 artificials from amongst the innumerable naturals floating on the water.

Although I had the flies to match the hatch, I didn't want to *battle* it: "Maybe a small emerger?"

Then, I remembered a propitious encounter of the previous day. We'd lunched with Vernon S. "Pete" Hidy. Pete, now long-since deceased, was a protegé of the late Jim Leisenring. He became a staunch proponent of the soft-hackled, fuzzy-bodied wet flies, called "flymphs," fished in ways to suggest emerging aquatic insects.

Pete tucked a small packet of these into my pocket as we said our goodbyes. "Give 'em a fair try," he said, eyes twinkling, "You may be in store for a surprise."

By the time I'd located the flymphs, Lee and Tommy were hard at it, not catching rainbows as fast as the other flyfishers in the stretch weren't catching them.

"What the heck," I thought, knotting a size 18 black flymph to a 6X tippet. For several minutes I'd been watching what appeared to be a good-sized rainbow feeding regularly, close to the opposing shoreline. The trout swirled, leaving a tantalizing hole in the water where a tiny dun had been trying to escape its shuck.

I angled a cast slightly down and across the current, cozying the flymph tight against the bank. As it approached the trout's lie, I jiggled the rod tip gently upward a few inches, then quickly dropped it to let slack, the technique Hidy had advised. He had suggested also that you should keep your eyes riveted to the floating part of the tippet while doing this. Most of the trout takes, he said, occurred after the lifting and dropping of the rod tip.

My tippet twitched! And I tightened up to find a fast-moving rainbow plowing downstream into a weed bed. Somehow, I managed to extricate that 15-inch fish and release it.

Another trout rose nearby. I cast and repeated the lifting and dropping tactic. The leader twitched once again. It was a larger trout that broke off when I set the hook too hard.

I tied on another flymph, this one two sizes larger and pale dun and yellowish in color. The difference in color and in size didn't affect the rainbows' interest in flymphs. Five more fish tumbled to the wiggly-hackled, fuzzy bodied flymph.

I left the water and hustled up Lee and Tommy, distributing what remained of the flymphs between the three of us. These flies ranged from size 20 through size 10, and included four distinctly different color combinations. Each of us hooked about twenty additional rainbows before leaving the river that evening.

Since that time, numerous similar experiences with rainbow trout have convinced me that the fly rarely is as important to these fish as the presentation and manipulation after it lands in the water.

Most fly fishers are aware that two main schools of fly selection exist, and that these are essentially "imitative" and "non-imitative" in their applications. Those who have spent a great deal of time fly fishing for trout, also tend to recognize that both methods produce consistent results under specific fishing circumstances.

The imitative approach attempts to closely simulate specific species of trout forage, insects and otherwise. If your fishing is limited to only a few waters, it is an especially favorable approach to fly selection, in that it limits the number of flies you need to carry.

One of the spring creeks mentioned earlier is a good example of where the imitative approach works best. One can carry an entire season's supply of flies in a single box containing four fly patterns. One is a caddis dry carried in three sizes, suggesting most of the caddis emerging from that stream across the season. Another dry represents the predominant species of mayflies. Another imitates the mayfly nymph. And, still another simulates the leech.

But using this approach isn't quite as practical if you intend to fish throughout a large geographic region in a wide variety of rainbow waters and for varieties of fish other than rainbows. A person fly fishing, for example, from Maryland to Maine, would be hard pressed to carry along imitative patterns for each rainbow, brown trout, brook trout, and landlocked salmon lake or stream he might fish in a single season. It would be impractical. Over a dozen fly boxes would be needed to tote along such a collection.

Many who fish this way, regionally, or over a broader expanse of North America, approach the problem from the viewpoint of carrying only those flies which have proven themselves to be *consistent* producers under varying conditions. It is a far more practical viewpoint from which to approach fly selection for the traveling angler. It assumes that even the best assortment of flies, effective in several geographic regions, will contain certain "gaps" that may need filling locally or at the portable fly-tying kit. What it allows is carrying along a *reasonable* selection of flies in no more than four fly boxes, which past experience has shown attract trout to them more often than not. Some of the flies may be imitative, others not. The criterion for selection is based solely on what the fly has done for the angler over a prolonged period of time under varying water conditions. It also assumes that the angler will tend to "weight" the selection somewhat in favor of the region where he does most of his fishing.

For those who flyfish for rainbows more often than they do for brown trout, this selection method tends to be nearly ideal. The reason that it is, is that rainbows are "free wheeling" feeders. They will often go for patterns of flies in one region that knock 'em dead elsewhere.

The practical, common sense fly-selection approach recognizes that certain fly patterns, such as the Adams, Muskrat Nymph, and Muddler Minnow suggest to the fish a raft of similar-appearing natural trout foods. It also recognizes the need to have available certain highly imitative ties. And, it also recognizes the benefits of the frequently simplified approach of the professional guide.

Flies suggesting freshwater leeches are among the most effective on rainbow trout. Pictured here are four of the author's favorites. Bottom, clockwise: *Wooly Bugger, Marabou Leech, Allan Robrer's Shady Lady, Gerlach's Leech, and the Blood Sucker (a Canadian pattern).*

In short, the commonsense selection of trout flies consists of patterns in which the angler has great *confidence,* based on past experience.

If your fishing tends to be local, perhaps the best way to start compiling a useful list is to chat with local fly fishers and fly shop owners. The question to them should be: "Which fly patterns do you consider to be *absolutely essential* to fishing this area?"

Another good way to go about it is to trust the regional fly patterns recommended by respected flyfishing writers. When I was a beginning fly fisher, flies recommended by Ted Trueblood, Joe Brooks, and Byron Dalrymple became integrated into my fly boxes. Some

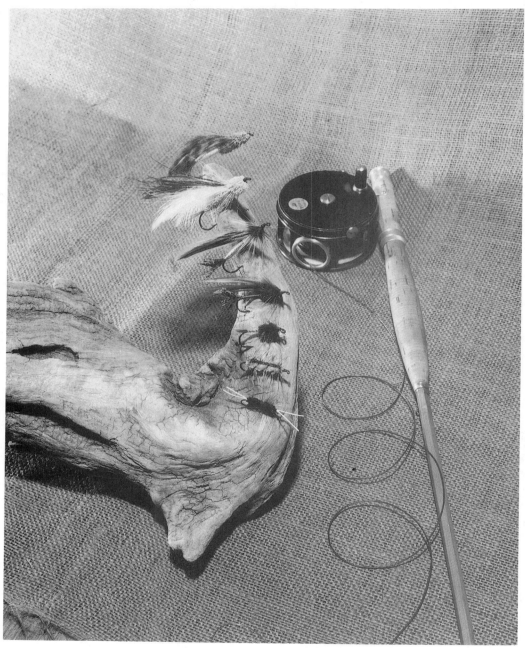

Being partial to catching large rainbows, the author frequently fishes with large streamers, wets, and nymphs. Some of those that have provided him plenty of action include (from top) Spuddler Minnow, Marabou Muddler, Silver Spruce, Spruce, Big Hole Demon, Wooly Worm, and Montana Nymph.

worked well for me. Others didn't. So I sorted them by on-the-water experience until arriving at the patterns I use today.

As my own list now stands, it reflects patterns selected because I have caught fish with them regularly wherever rainbows, browns, cutthroats, Arctic grayling, and steelheads are found. I will be the first to admit that it has a western flavor, reflecting my present-day fly fishing as angling editor of *Western Outdoors Magazine*, which circulates in the eleven western states.

The patterns that I consider to be most useful today are *not* all the same ones I preferred while living in other regions. They have changed to reflect a more national flavor.

That list follows for the benefit of the newcomer to rainbow fly fishing. Identified with each pattern are the general type of insect or other forage suggested by the fly. Also included is the size range in which I carry each pattern.

Nymphs, Wet Flies, Streamer Flies (2 boxes)

Bird's Nest (pupating caddis, sizes 12, 10, 3XL)

Bitch Creek (stonefly nymphs, sizes 10–6, 3XL)

Black Rubberlegs (stonefly nymph, sizes 8–2, 2XL)

Black Dragonfly Nymph (dragonfly nymph, sizes 8, 6, 2XL)

Black A. P. Nymph (mayfly nymph, sizes 18, 16)

Brassie (caddis or midge pupa, sizes 18–14)

Gray Hackle, peacock (mayfly nymph or caddis pupa, sizes 14–8)

Hare's Ear Nymph (mayfly nymph, sizes 16–10)

Heather Nymph (damselfly nymph, sizes 12, 10, 3XL)

Marabou Leech (leech, black/gray/olive variants, sizes 10, 8, 3XL)

O'Gara Shrimp (scud, size 6)

Olive Dragonfly Nymph (dragonfly nymph, size 6, 2XL)

Rosborough's Muskrat Nymph (midge pupa, sizes 16–10, 2XL)

Royal Trude (attractor, sizes 16–2)

San Juan Worm (waterworm, sizes 8, 6)

Spuddler Minnow (sculpin minnow, sizes 6–2, 3XL)

Telico Nymph (nymph, sizes 16–10)

White Marabou Muddler (minnow, sizes 6–2, 3XL)

Wooly Bugger (leech, sizes 10–4, 3XL)

Yellow Marabou Muddler (perch minnow, sizes 6–2, 3XL)

Dry Flies, Emergers (2 boxes)

Adams (generic mayfly, sizes 18–10)

Bird's Stonefly (Pteronarcys c. stonefly, sizes 6–2, 3XL)

Black Ant (ant, sizes 18–10)

Black Beetle (beetle, sizes 12–8)

Black Hannah (mayfly, sizes 16, 14)

Brown Ant (midge, ant, sizes 16, 14)

Elk Hair Caddis (caddis, sizes 16–10)

Gray Caddis Emerger (caddis, sizes 16–10)

Gray Wulff (mayfly, sizes 14–10)

Joe's Hopper (grasshopper, sizes 12, 10, 3XL)

Mosquito (mosquito, sizes 16, 14)

Olive-bodied Comparadun (Baetid mayfly, sizes 16–10)

Olive Caddis Emerger (caddis, sizes 10, 8)

Pale Cream/Tan Parachute (Callibaetis mayfly, sizes 18, 16)

Royal Trude (attractor, sizes 16–8)

Tom Thumb (hatched "traveling sedge" caddis, sizes 8, 6)

Yellow-bodied Humpy (mayfly, sizes 14–10)

These are the patterns which produced over ninety percent of the trout, rainbows and otherwise, which I have caught over the past forty-eight years. (Bear in mind I've been fly fishing since the age of nine). They are the patterns I've come to count on to produce *consistent* fishing for resident rainbows wherever I have sought them, West, Midwest, or East.

Selecting a list of effective steelhead flies is even easier. Regardless of what one may have read or heard from others, the truth is that steelheads are as easy to attract to the fly as the most gullible resident rainbows. What's important here is having a range of color combinations that can be seen by the fish in clear or tinted water, and in overcast or sunny weather. It's also important to stock these patterns in a range of sizes and in tying styles for low- and high-water conditions.

My experience parallels that of numerous other steelheaders with regard to pattern selection. And that is, if you can get a fly sufficiently close to a steelhead, the fish will come to it. I have experimented by changing patterns between hook-ups often enough to be convinced the color of the fly makes little differ-

The author feels that few steelhead fly patterns are needed to catch fish consistently, but that carrying the patterns in a range of sizes and styles for low- to high-water conditions is important. This low-water tie is used in very clear summer-run streams when the water's down.

The Skunk steelhead bucktail, and its green-butted variant, the Green-Butted Skunk are ranked high on the author's list of preferred steelhead flies.

ence when steelheads are biting. However, certain color combinations seem more visible to them when the water's tinted or turbid. Some color combinations also seem to be more attractive early and late in the day, others at midday.

Those flies having combinations of black and white have been most deadly for me, regardless of light conditions and water clarity, with the Skunk topping

the list. In midday under bright light, patterns having yellow, orange, or red in them have produced the best. Purple seems to be a deadly color both in clear and off-color water. Neutral shades, such as those in the Riffle Dancer and Muddler Minnow, bring steelheads readily to the surface when the water temperature is suitable. All black, or a combination of black and yellow or black and orange—such as the Black Gordon, Ward's Wasp,

One of the author's favorite late-in-the-day steelhead flies is the Black and Orange Marabou, a Spey-type steelhead fly introduced to him by professional guide J. D. Love of Beaver, Washington.

For winter-run steelhead fly fishing, the author tends to favor bright patterns containing some fluorescent coloring when the water is tinged. This one is the Sol Duc, Spey, dressed on a size 2/0 hook.

and Black/Orange Marabou (dressed Spey style)—have been consistent producers very late in the day. Spey-type dressings, often in fluorescent shades and large sizes, are as consistent on winter-runs as any I have found.

My personal list follows. These will fit into two large fly boxes in the sizes I normally carry.

Steelhead Flies (2 boxes)
   Black Gordon (sizes 8–4)
   Black/Orange Marabou, Spey (sizes 6–1/0)
   Black/Purple Marabou, Spey (sizes 4–2/0)
   Blue Charm (both low-water and bucktail, sizes 8–4)
   Fall Favorite (sizes 8–1/0)
   Golden Demon (sizes 10–4)
   Green-Butted Skunk (sizes 6–2)
   Muddler Minnow (sizes 10–6)
   Royal Coachman Bucktail (sizes 10–4)
   Skunk (sizes 10–1/0)
   Ward's Wasp (size 8–2)

These additional patterns are occasionally brought along, depending upon water clarity and temperature.

   Brindle Bug (sizes 10–6)
   Cole's Comet (sizes 6–2)

Double Flame Egg (sizes 8–2)
Juicy Bug (size 10 double)
Orange Herron (sizes 4–2/0)
Painted Lady (sizes 6–2)
Riffle Dancer (sizes 4–2)
Quilloyute (sizes 2–3/0)
Sol Duc (sizes 2–3/0)

Sol Duc, Dark (sizes 4–2/0)
Sol Duc, Spey (sizes 2–3/0)

The chapters of the book that follow are about how to put these and all the other flies to best use.

6

Stream Tactics

This chapter and the one following it are directed to helping the reader put the "bite" into the rainbow and steelhead fishing strategies presented in earlier chapters. Consistently successful rainbow tactics are strongly affected by what you do before and after stepping into the water. Although the fish are relatively easy to bring to the fly, keeping them on the hook can be quite another matter. The tackle and rigging used and the methods by which fish are played can affect the outcome, more than for any other species of trout. Great attention to detail is needed, starting with selecting proper tackle and rigging, and ending with leading the fish to the beach.

Tackle Selection

Choosing the ideal rods, reels, lines, and leaders for successful rainbow and steelhead fishing is altogether as important as it is in seeking out brown trout or Atlantic salmon. Although we are dealing with trout which often are much easier to bring to the fly, these are fish with startling speed and staying power. You need terminal rigs that will stand the test, as well as rods, reels, and lines capable of dealing with a great variety of conditions. Equipment that is both *versatile* and *strong* is critical, if one is truly serious about catching rainbow trout larger than "pan" size.

Fly Rods

My own experiences have indicated that the "ideal" fly rods are those that allow you to cope comfortably with whatever conditions exist on a given

Bud Lilly tests this beautiful spring creek.

Professional guide Mark Daly fishing an ideal rainbow trout run on the Madison River.

stretch of water. Scaling of the tackle to the conditions results in versatility in presentation.

Like most long-time fly fishers, I have accumulated more rods than I'd need for five lifetimes. For rainbow and steelhead fly fishing, I fish mainly with less than a half-dozen. Of these rods, only a couple are my mainstays on larger rivers. These are 9-footers carrying 6-, 7-, or 8-weight lines. On spring creeks and tunnel streams, I fish with rods carrying 3- to 5-weight lines, depending on the severity of the wind. For small, brushy streams I use 7- to 7½-foot rods. Where there is plenty of casting room behind me, I opt for 9-footers.

Since my own fishing is primarily

on western waters—many of which are open, big water—fishing for resident rainbows involves using a 9-foot Scott for 6-weight, a 9-foot Orvis Western for 6-weight, and an early Scientific Anglers System 7, which accommodates both 7- and 8-weight lines. These are the rods I feel comfortable and confident using.

The point here is not which brand of fly rod is best, for most are quite good in these days. A person should become so familiar with the feel and performance of a certain rod that little concentration on it is needed while fishing. Fishing with too great a selection of rods defeats this purpose.

For rainbow and steelhead fishing, ninety percent can be effectively accomplished with three rods. Limit the selection to the few that suit you best. These are the rods that consistently allow you to do what you want with the fly line and the hooked fish.

If you are a veteran fly fisher, you already know which rods are right for the fishing you do.

For the beginner, the following selection chart is provided to serve as a guideline.

The newest graphite materials, such as IMX and IM6, produce rods capable of delivering extremely fast line speeds. Faster line speeds permit casting heavier flies on lighter-weight lines than was considered feasible only a decade ago. This, in turn, has caused many anglers to completely reevaluate the weights of lines they use.

In the past, many fishermen felt (correctly) that 8- and 9-weight lines were the ideal ones for casting considerable distances with large streamer flies in the wind. Today, many—including this writer—find that they can accomplish equal deliveries of the fly using 6- and 7-weight lines with the up-to-date graphite rods. The advantages of the lighter,

Size of Stream	Wind Condition	Surrounding Conditions	Rod Lengths	Line Weights
Small	Windy	Brushy	7'-7½'	4, 5, 6
Small	Still	Brushy	7'-7½'	2, 3, 4
Small	Windy	Open	7½'-8½'	5, 6
Small	Still	Open	7½'-8½'	2, 3, 4
Medium	Windy	Brushy	7½'-9'	4, 5, 6
Medium	Still	Brushy	7½'-9'	2, 3, 4
Medium	Windy	Open	8'-9'	4, 5, 6
Medium	Still	Open	8'-9'	2, 3, 4
Large	Windy or still	Open or brushy	8½'-9'	6, 7*, 8*, 9*

* These rods are for casting wind-resistant, large trout and steelhead flies.

faster fly rods are most felt at the end of several days of intensive fishing.

Reels

If I had the option of living a second lifetime, I'd probably decide to spend it as a fly reel designer. Very few reels satisfy my needs when fishing for rainbows and steelheads. Among present-day fly reels, price doesn't necessarily assure the

kind of performance that suits rainbow and steelhead fishing.

Perhaps the most important quality needed in a fly reel is a *finely-adjustable, smooth-running* drag system. Although some of the reels in my collection cost me triple-digit dollars for the privilege of using, few compare without drag-modification to the first reel my father gave me as a youngster: a Pfleuger model 1495½. At that time, it cost Dad about fifteen dollars. But the drag can be ad-

A smooth-running drag system is essential in a fly reel for rainbow trout and steelhead fishing. The author's preferences include the Orvis Presentation model EXR with an exposed rim.

The System Two model 78-L fly reel, manufactured in England for Scientific Anglers/3M, has fast-starting, smooth-running drag characteristics. Like the Orvis Presentation reel, it has a counter-balanced spool to offset vibration during a sustained run by a big 'bow.

justed to scant ounces of smooth tensioning. Though the finish of that reel is practically worn off from use, I often select it in preference to more expensive reels to tangle with large, fast-moving rainbows.

More recently, I have acquired a couple of additional reels not requiring drag-system modifications before being suitable for rainbow trout fishing. The best of these, in my opinion, is the Orvis Presentation model for 7- and 8-weight lines. It is machined to extremely close tolerances. The spools do not wobble on the pillar-shaft. The drag system can be quickly adjusted to a heavier or lighter tension.

Scientific Anglers new System Two lightweights offer suitable drag adjustment and smooth-running characteristics.

The second most important characteristic of a fly reel is that extra spools are available. I recommend purchasing no less than four extra spools for each reel. You'll need them to have fast access to the selection of fly lines needed for versatility on the water. Purchase a second complete reel, if you can afford it, so that a replacement is available if you break or lose the reel. It's a good idea on trips to remote wilderness areas.

Select fly reel size to suit the weights of lines you need plus adequate backing to handle the rainbow's powerful, sustained runs. On small streams, 25 to 50 yards of 20-pound-test Cortland Micron backing line will be more than enough. On larger rivers holding resident rainbows, 100 to 150 yards of 20-pound-test backing line is adequate. When fishing for steelheads in the 15- to 30-pound class, 200 yards of backing line will give you a better margin of safety.

Fly reel weight should be selected to properly balance with the weight of the rod being used. This should be determined using a reel spooled with both backing line and fly line. The reel should not be so light as to cause the rod to feel excessively tip-heavy, nor so heavy as to distribute excessive weight at the rod's butt. The entire outfit should have a nicely balanced feel about it when resting in the casting hand.

Lines

Versatility should be the aim of the fly fisher selecting lines for rainbow trout. You'll need to be able to fish from the water's surface to the bottom. On larger rivers, you may need floating, sink-tip, slow-sinking, fast-sinking, and extra-fast-sinking lines.

When I am not certain of the water conditions on a given stream, I'll carry at least five different lines on extra spools.

Here, Bud Lilly used a floating line to hook a nice rainbow feeding on caddis in the Madison River in Montana.

A Hi-D shooting head accounted for this beautiful 10-pound "hen" steelhead. The fish was caught on a Skunk steelhead bucktail.

This eliminates the need to re-spool to a different kind of line at streamside, thus wasting valuable fishing time.

On waters having very stable water-level conditions, I know in advance exactly which lines I'll require. For example, on the Fall River—a large spring creek in northern California—I carry three lines: a floater, a fast-sinking sink-tip, and an extra-fast-sinking Wet Head. A trip to the huge Clearwater River in Idaho, on the other hand, means I'll have to carry along a floating bug-taper, a Hi-D sink-tip bug-taper, and three sink-rates of sinking shooting-taper lines. By way of comparison, a day's jaunt to my favorite

local southern California trout stream requires only a floating fly line to probe its shallow reaches with dry flies and nymphs.

Tactical versatility on the stream comes from having a selection of fly lines spooled on reels and ready to meet whatever conditions might be encountered. With only six lines (a floater; a fast-sinking sink-tip; a Hi-D Wet Head; and fast-, extra-fast, and Super-Sinker shooting tapers), one could cope with practically any stream or river condition in the United States or Canada.

However, if you rarely venture far from a certain region, the selection should be scaled to the waters regularly fished. If you're planning a trip to an unfamiliar area, local guides and outfitters should be consulted with to determine any additional lines that might be required.

Leaders

Leaders varying from 3 to 15 feet will cover most rainbow trout stream fishing situations. For steelhead fishing, leaders from 3 to 7½ feet are likely to suffice. Tippet sizes ranging from 7X to 0X will handle both types of fishing because an extensive range of fly sizes and weights are required in most regions.

Knotless tapered leaders pick up less weed than knotted leaders when fishing spring creeks. The short three- to five-foot leaders used for sinking line fishing have to be home-tied. One can experiment to achieve tapers which turn over properly when cast, or follow the recommendations offered by leader material suppliers, such as Orvis. Leaders normally suitable for rainbow fishing in streams are equally applicable to lake fishing for them.

The angler who ties his own leaders has an advantage. The ability to tie or modify leaders *skillfully* gives tactical versatility on the water. Minor adjustments in leaders can alter presentations—how the fly floats on the current or runs below the surface. I will discuss the importance of correct leader design for specific tactical presentations a bit later on.

Accessories

Anyone walking into a well-stocked fly tackle shop will quickly recognize that it might be all too easy to accumulate over a thousand dollars worth of flyfishing accessories. I won't even mention the wealth of accessories for fly tying.

The ones a person really *needs* to fly fish effectively for trout can be easily tucked into a single pocket in the fly fishing vest. These include a clipper to nip tag ends off leader knots, a tiny pliers to pinch down hook barbs, a small piece of rubber to straighten leaders, a hook file, fly floatant, leader-sink, and line dressing. There are two additional aids that are *absolutely* essential to tactical versatility in rainbow trout fishing: strike indicators and tiny, lead split-shot, pinch-ons or twist-ons.

Strike Indicators

The purpose of a strike indicator is simply to enhance your ability to detect the trout's sometimes delicate take of a nymph. Oftentimes, the rainbow's inhaling of a drifting nymph will be so delicate that it merely causes the leader to twitch slightly where it enters the water. Sometimes, the indication of the take may be even more subtle, such as an instant of hesitation in the drifting of the fly.

Two basic types of strike indicators have evolved to aid anglers in seeing these subtle acceptances by the trout. One type of strike indicator is a highly visible leader butt or line tip. This is used for "high-sticking" a nymph upstream on a short line to achieve a bottom-bouncing drift. High-sticking is without doubt, one of the two deadliest techniques for attracting rainbows to nymph flies in relatively shallow riffles and boulder-formed pocket water.

In this fishing, even though less than

20 feet of line and leader may be used to make the presentation, flat or dim light may make it difficult to see the leader hestitate as the fly drifts back toward you following the upstream delivery.

One of the best ways to aid your ability to detect a hesitation in the tip of the line or leader butt is to replace the leader's butt-section with a section of fluorescent red or chartreuse leader material. Both colors tend to be highly visible when in low light conditions. At least one manufacturer offers "hot-butt" leaders for sale. Most fly shops stock the fluorescent Ashaway Amnesia and Cortland Plion monofilaments from which they can be home-tied. (These materials also can be used as shooting lines in conjunction with shooting-taper fly lines.)

Both Cortland Line Company and Scientific Anglers/3M offer full length fluorescent fly lines that enhance visibility under poor lighting conditions. Cortland also has designed a floating line with a short tip of bright fluorescent red. It is called a Nymph Tip line. Both the Nymph Tip and all-fluorescent fly lines are useful when high-sticking nymphs upstream.

The second main kind of strike indicator is intended to signal the take of a fly with the indicator floating along on the surface. These take several forms, including the tuft of polypropylene yarn

The floating, plastic-foam strike-indicator is pinched onto the leader anywhere the angler wants it. It is held in place with an adhesive that grips when the indicator is pinched on.

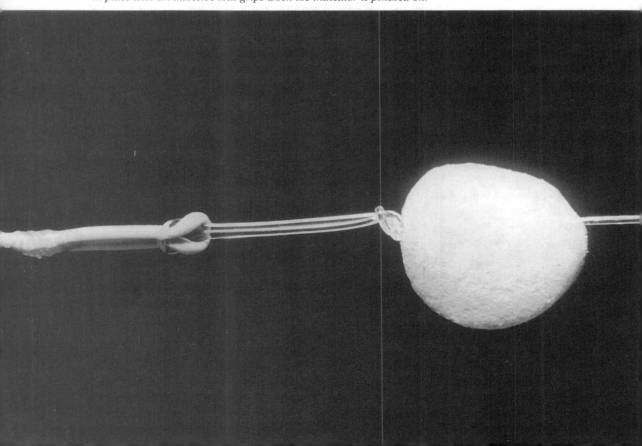

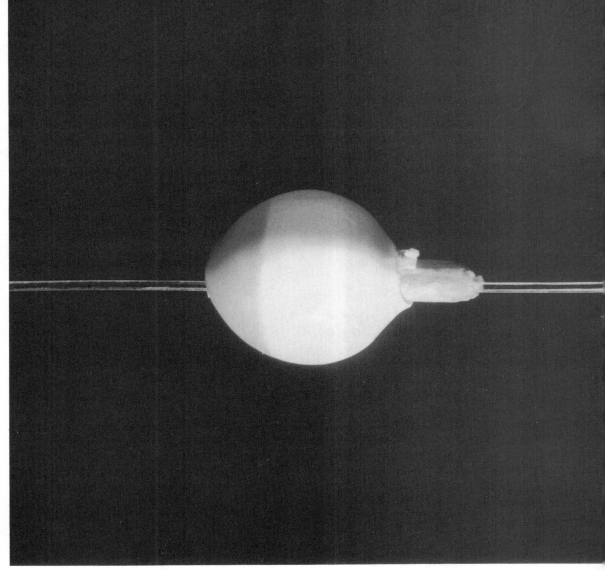

Corkies are actually miniaturized "bobbers" designed as strike indicators for fly fishing. The leader is run through the hole in the middle of the corkie, then it is pegged into place with a piece of round toothpick.

knotted to the tippet described in an earlier chapter.

Others are made from floating plastic-foam tabs. These have an adhesive backing that lets you pinch them on the leader wherever you want. Orvis and Palsa Products are among several manufacturers offering the tabs for sale through fly shops. They come in a selection of bright, fluorescent colors.

Another type of floating strike indicator is called a corkie. What it amounts to is a minute bobber that's run up the leader and pegged into place with a piece of round toothpick.

The advantages of corkies are several.

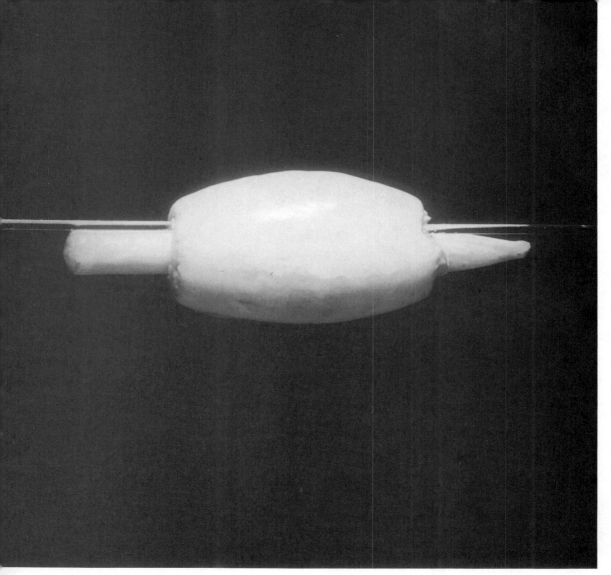

Floating strike indicators can be made from scrap cork. The author makes these in sizes larger than corkies for fishing very large, weighted nymphs.

For one thing, you can easily adjust the indicator's position along the leader to adapt to different depths of water being fished. The larger corkies will also suspend relatively large, weighted nymphs beneath them without being pulled beneath the surface.

Some anglers, who, like me, fish very large size 4 and 2 weighted nymphs, will fashion even larger, more buoyant indicators out of pieces of scrap fly-rod handle cork rings. On these, I simply "burn" a hole through the center of the formed cork, using a heated needle slightly smaller than the diameter of my leader butt. I finish the indicator with a coat of white lacquer, followed by two coats of fluorescent lacquer, giving it a final clear coat for protection.

Polypropylene yarn of a fluorescent red color is my favorite strike indicator for fishing flat-running spring creeks and irrigation ditches. Being light as a feather, it casts more delicately than a corkie or plastic-foam indicator. I clinch it directly into a leader knot or tie it into a long tippet to form a *right-angle connection* to the nymph below, by means of an improved clinch knot. On slow-moving stretches (and in lakes, too!) this right-angle connection provides an un-bellied tippet between the nymph and

Tufts of polypropylene fly-tying yarn in fluorescent colors are ideal strike indicators. They're easy to cast and can be knotted into a tippet to form a right-angle attachment using the improved clinch knot. The yarn indicator is saturated with fly flotant to keep it riding high in the water.

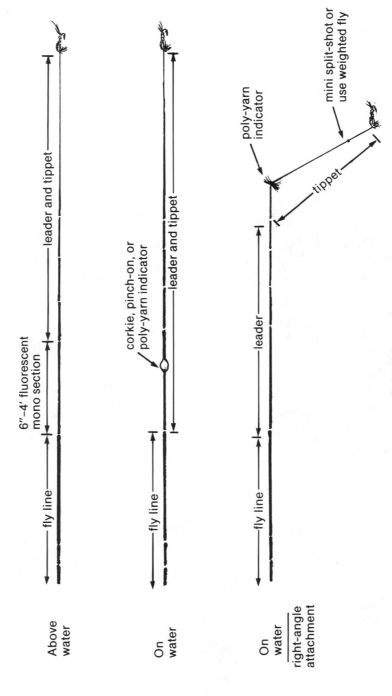

Strike-indicator placement.

the yarn-indicator. This results in being able to detect the light take of the fish more quickly. And that is especially helpful to those of us, who, though we may not yet qualify for senior citizen discounts, have discovered our eyesight and reaction times to be not quite what they used to be.

Leader-Weighting Leads

Faster-flowing stream currents sometimes necessitate using either heavily weighted flies or tiny weights pinched onto the leader to keep the nymph or streamer fly from riding up in the current. These come in several forms. Some are made from soft lead in both split-shot and slotted linear forms. Others are made from hard lead that grips the leader more firmly than those made from soft lead. Others, come in the form of soft-lead strips that are twisted around the leader above leader knots. They all work as intended. I carry all three in my fly fishing vest when fishing for resident trout. For steelhead fishing, I'll normally carry only the hard-lead split-shot, which stay on the leader better when making powerful casts. You'll get a better feel of how and where to use them later in this chapter.

Basic Line and Leader Rigs for Rainbow Fishing

Correct rigging is essential to make the most out of the presentation techniques decided upon for a given stretch of water. In this section, I'll describe the most important riggings for rainbows and steelheads. Knowing how to assemble these correctly greatly enhances your on-the-water versatility.

Select a leader taper having good turn-over characteristics. Turnover should occur in a straight, fully extended manner from the tip of the fly line.

Choose a leader butt that is roughly the same flexibility as the tip of the fly line being used. A butt section significantly more pliant or stiff than the line tip is almost certain to hinge upon being cast. Hinging interrupts the smooth transfer of energy through the line and into the leader. A severe crack in the line, where it's attached to the leader's butt, will have a similar effect.

Leader materials vary greatly in stiffness from brand to brand. As a result, judging the stiffness is a matter of "feel," until one discovers which brands of leaders are the most suitable for your casting. I go about this by grasping the line tip between thumbs and forefingers of each hand about three inches apart. Then I gently flex the line. I repeat this process using the leader material, until I feel the two flex similarly. Then I string a fly rod and test the combination on the front lawn.

If the line is brand new, another step usually is in order. Some lines are designed with tip sections which need trimming back before they cast properly. To check this out, I'll take a leader which I know to have good turnover characteristics and nail knot it to the line tip. If the line and leader are not turning over correctly, I'll start cutting back the line tip a half-inch at a time until they do. On modern American and British fly lines, rarely more than four inches of line tip need to be removed.

Once this is accomplished, I'll make a more permanent attachment, usually an internal nail knot or loop of heavy mono spliced into the line tip. Then I will retest the line and leader to assure myself that I won't have to fight improper turnover when I'm fishing.

Doing this not only improves one's ability to achieve die-straight casts out on the water, but it also eliminates one of the possible distractions to concentrating on the fishing. It adds *consistency* to the tactical approach, much in the same way as having a tennis racquet strung to the correct tension for the player adds consistency to that game.

The method by which the leader butt is attached to the fly line also affects turnover. Any attachment which concentrates excess weight at the attachment-point between line and leader butt may achieve greater velocity than the line or leader, causing a hinging effect. The ideal attachment method, therefore, strives to keep the weight at the joining-point to a minimum.

Without a doubt, the worst possible attachment of line tip to leader butt is a figure-eight or clinch knot of the line tip to a loop tied in the leader's butt-end.

The ideal attachment involves either running the leader butt end into the line tip and epoxying it there, or slipping a short length of braided mono leader over the line tip and affixing it with epoxy. Special kits for doing both are available in fly shops.

Braided-butt leaders offer what may be the stronger alternative of the two. These slide easily over the line tip and can be held firmly there with a miniscule plastic collar for temporary use. A drop of epoxy cement makes the attachment a permanent one.

I prefer an even stronger attachment when fishing large flies for big trout and steelheads. For this I use the internal nail knot. In this, the leader butt is inserted into a hole up the line core, formed by a hot needle. The needle is worked cold for an inch or two up the line core. Then it's pushed through the line's outer wall. The needle is then heated to make the hole permanent. This creates a hole through which to pass a length of leader butt material long enough for knotting.

A nail knot is then tied on the line *above* the hole through which the leader butt was passed. This knot is then saturated with a bonding cement, such as Flexament, or a smooth-drying plastic, like Aquaseal. This both bonds the mono firmly to the line and itself, and when applied in sufficient coatings, provides a smooth-surfaced connection to slide easily through the guides.

This attachment does create somewhat more bulk at the joint than may be desired by those fishing very light lines and fine leaders on spring creeks. Modest hinging sometimes takes place. For those situations, where fine tippets are used and finesse employed in handling hooked rainbows, I myself prefer the braided-butt or epoxied internal joints. Far better leader turnover and presentational delicacy can be achieved by using them, in my opinion.

Methods of rigging strike indicators were discussed earlier in the chapter. As a result, because illustrations showing their attachment accompany the descriptions, there's no need here to review them. The same does not apply to the use of leader-weighting leads. Using these correctly requires additional commentary and clear illustrations of how to go about it.

Weighting Leads

The use of weighted flies, or leads placed onto the leader to hold unweighted flies down in the current, re-

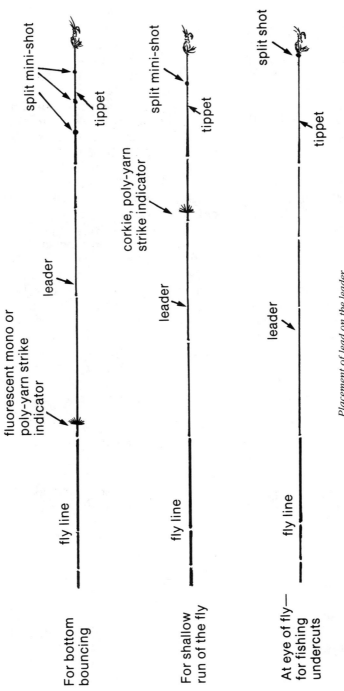

Placement of lead on the leader.

lates to what sort of presentation the angler seeks to achieve. Three objectives come to mind for weighting flies and leaders.

The first is to achieve an instantaneous sinking of the fly into a pocket along an undercut bank. It's a commonly used method of probing undercut banks from drifting boats on large rivers and from wading positions in smaller streams.

Two types of sunken flies are most often used in this tactic: those representing nymphs or crayfish, and those which are dressed to look like forage fish or fry. In both instances, the attempt is to get the fly deep and quickly enough to attract a trout lying under or close by the undercut.

There are a couple of very logical ways in which to do this. One simply is to weight the fly so heavily that it sinks like a rock when it hits the water. When fishing from a drifting boat, where repeated casts may be made to the bank throughout the day, the heavily weighted fly is most ideal. Montana guide, Mark Daly, for example, epoxys lead "eyes" to the head of the fly, over-wraps the joint with crisscross thread wraps, then coats the wrappings with more epoxy. This assures that the eyes stay in place. Flies dressed with the largest, $1/18$-ounce lead eyes fish more like spinning jigs—but they get down fast. And that is what is needed to get them in front of fish lurking in the stream's undercut zone.

The alternative, of course, is to pinch on from one to three hard lead split-shot at the juncture of the fly head and tippet. These tend to be rather easily stripped from the tippet when fighting hooked fish and when they encounter underwater obstructions, such as tree limbs. As a result, close attention needs to be paid to

the shot on the leader each time the fly is lifted from the water following a cast and retrieval. Doing this tends to break my concentration on the actual fishing. Thus, I prefer using the flies tied with the heavy lead eyes.

A second reason for deploying lead on the leader is to bottom-bounce the nymph along the streambed. To accomplish this, the high-sticking method is ideal in water shallow enough to wade. In other situations, an up-and-across delivery may be needed, as when probing deeper current edges adjacent to wadeable water. A similar tactic also is adaptable to fishing crayfish-imitators along rocky river ledges.

Rigging the fly to bottom-bounce involves accurately estimating the depth of the water through which the fly will pass. For upstream deliveries, start by pinching one tiny split-shot onto the tippet six to twelve inches from the fly. Make a presentation, noting whether or not the fly regularly ticks the bottom during the downstream drift. If it doesn't, add another split shot to the tippet nine inches above the first one. Cast again. If the fly ticks the bottom regularly, don't add any more weight. If it does not, continue adding split-shot to the leader at nine-inch intervals, until the fly regularly comes into contact with the stream bottom.

Be advised that no matter how cautiously one adds split-shot to the leader, considerable numbers of flies will be lost using this technique. The flies hook streambed snags and become lodged in the rocks. The technique is deadly, but you pay the price for it in lost flies and scuffed and tangled leaders.

Another important application of split-shot to the leader is when a floating strike indicator is used to drift the fly along without contacting the streambed. It's done exactly as in high-sticking rigs, except that the weight of the shot must be light enough to prevent pulling the strike indicator under the water. In this rig, the weight of the minute split-shot simply keeps the fly from billowing up towards the surface under the indicator. It's deadly with mayfly nymphs.

Rigging Sink-Tip Fly Lines

Sink-tip lines are among the most useful when stream fishing. This is due mainly to the rainbow's free-wheeling feeding and tendency to frequent "slots" in the current and rocky pockets where a great deal of line mending is needed to obtain a correct run of the sunken fly.

The sink-tip line is called that because the front five to ten feet of line sink, while the rest remains floating.

Sink-tip lines are available in both fast-sinking and extra-fast-sinking types. The sink-rate selection depends on the depth and flow of the water being fished. Versatility is increased by having both available.

In stream situations, the sink-tip fly line is best suited to fishing slots and runs of shallow to moderate depth and moderate current speed. These are the kinds of waters where having only the short, front-end of the line sink is more advantageous than having thirty feet of sinking line, as in the Wet-Head or shooting taper.

Sink-tip lines also are sometimes effective in probing slow-moving pools and runs in which damselfly and dragonfly nymphs may be on the move. Some prefer them in shallow stretches of tailwaters and spring creeks harboring leeches and forage fish.

The sink-tip line's greatest versatility will be experienced when fishing medium- to large-sized trout streams. They are also extremely useful in summer-run and winter-run steelhead fishing under low, clear water conditions.

In most stream situations requiring their use, the sink-tip lines are selected for their ability to get the fly down fast next to an undercut bank, or to run it through a slot of fast water that is deeper and more turbulent than adjoining currents. And in these situations, a leader from two to six feet long may be adviseable. Longer leaders don't sink the fly as quickly as short ones.

When fishing the deep undercut from a wading position, you may want to further assure the fly's staying deep by using a heavily weighted fly or pinching split-shot onto the tippet near the head of the fly.

On rarer occasions, such as when trying to "undulate" a leech fly through a backwater eddy, the more effective presentation will be made with a long, unweighted leader and fly. The objective in this situation is to undulate the leech somewhat off the bottom. And it is one of those times when having the ability to modify one's leader offers a tactical advantage.

Rigging Full-length Sinking Fly Lines and Wet Heads

The full-length sinking fly line is *not* the most effective line with which to explore deep-running stream waters. The reason is that once the line sinks it can't be mended to control the run of the fly.

A better line for doing this is the Scien-

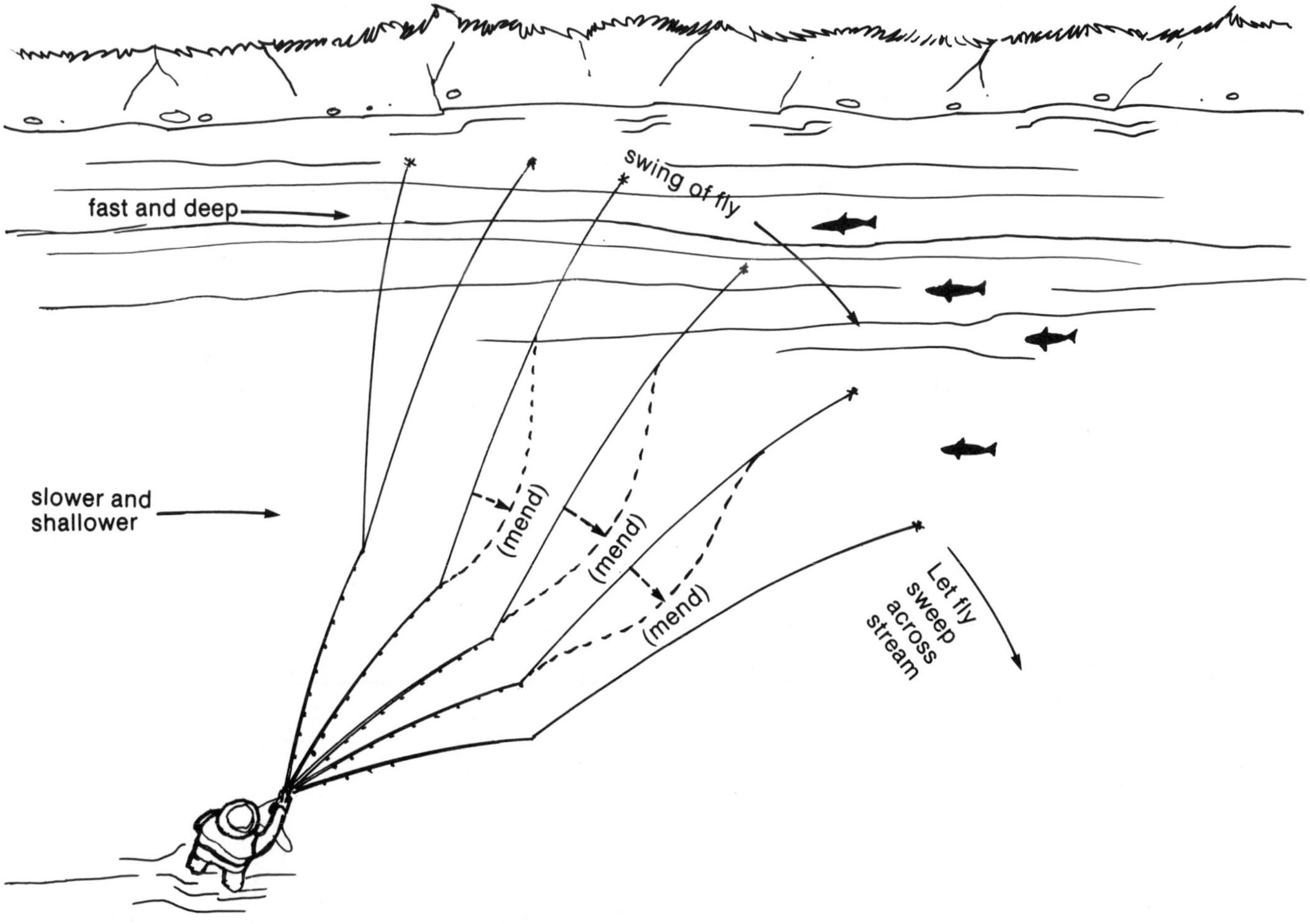

Let fly
sweep
across
stream

Swing of fly

(mend)

(mend)

(mend)

fast and deep

slower and
shallower

Using the sink-tip line to fish a deep channel.

tific Anglers Wet Head, or a shooting head backed by floating shooting-line. The Wet Head is a line in which the front 30-foot sinking section is integral with the running line. No knotting is required between the two, as in rigging a shooting taper.

In practice, the Wet Head fishes much like a shooting taper. Because the running line floats, mending tactics can be employed to give the fly a downstream drift broadside to the current. In this presentation, *more* fly is visible to the fish than when it's offered quartering or tail-end first.

I am not unique in experiencing that the broadside drift is one of the better presentations when seeking to provoke responses from both resident rainbows and the more easily "triggered" steelheads. Floating, sink-tip, Wet Head, and shooting-taper fly lines all accomplish the broadside drift superbly, depending on how deeply you need to fish.

As in rigging the sink-tip line, the shorter the leader, the more deeply the fly will run. Leaders from three to five feet long serve most of my purposes wherever I'm fishing. The leader attachment to the line should be a strong one, since great stress often is put on it by hooking the river bottom and trying to break loose. The powerful fighting ability of large rainbows and steelheads also requires the strongest joint possible. This also applies to the full-sinking line when it may be needed to fish a certain type of water effectively.

Shooting-taper lines are leader-rigged similarly to sink-tips and Wet Heads for deep-water stream fishing. The difference lies in the attachment of the "head" to a free-running type of monofilament or floating shooting-line. Greater casting distance than possible with conventional lines is achieved by means of the double haul casting technique. The amount of shooting-line needed to extend the cast is peeled off the reel into a stripping basket, or allowed to trail in long loops from the lips or hand of the caster. This line is released as the final "kick" is applied to the casting stroke. The weight of the shooting taper pulls the shooting-line through the guides.

The shooting taper is a 30-foot fly line, tapered to the tip much like a double-tapered line cut off 30 feet from its tip section. It is attached to the shooting-line by one of several methods. These include a direct splice into the large end of the head, a loop-to-loop attachment of head to shooting-line, or a knotting of the monofilament to a braided loop spliced into the butt of the head. Some employ an internal nail knot of the mono to the fly line.

All these attachment methods *work*. But the bulkier ones tend to be difficult to work out through the guides as you prepare to cast. My own preference tends towards the strongest attachment, the internal nail knot. It is less convenient when one wants to change from one sink-rate of shooting taper to another, however. Most anglers needing to make this change periodically in a day of fishing opt for the clinch knot to braided loop method. Others, like me, use an external nail knot between the shooting mono and the head. The choice between the methods lies mainly in the preference of the individual angler.

Lead-core Shooting Tapers

On occasion, the angler will want to use a shooting-taper line that sinks drastically faster than conventional shooting tapers. One can create these out of lengths of 18- to 25-pound-test lead-core trolling line, or purchase factory-made lines that are easier to cast.

The factory-made Cannonball, Deep Water Express, and Super Sinker shooting tapers are attached to the shooting-line by the methods previously described. The home-made lead-core head is attached by means of an external nail knot. When this latter knot is used for long periods of time, its permanency is better assured by a coat or two of Flexament or Aquaseal.

Types of Stream and River Water

For flyfishing purposes, there are six types of water moving through a stream that can be clearly defined. Taking them progressively, from the slowest flowing to the fastest, these are: pools, meanders, pockets, riffles, runs, and rapids.

How one presents a fly to a rainbow lying in any of them depends on the type of natural trout food the fly represents and the way the current influences the run of the fly once it's on or in the water.

Pools

As indicated in the chapter concerning prime stream locations for rainbows, the slow-moving waters of the pool can be viewed as consistently productive for rainbow trout. The reason they can, of course, is that pools often contain both a great variety and abundance of natural food organisms.

Rainbow trout in pools tend to be both aggressive and wary. The reason they're often wary is that the surface of the pool is frequently unbroken. As a result, the fish can readily detect movements made by the angler. Any presentation made by casting the leader or fly line over their window of vision through the water is likely to put the fish down.

Ideally a surface or near-surface presentation of a fly to a pool rainbow should come from somewhere well upstream of the fish. If the fly is dressed to suggest a relatively immobile mayfly dun or spinner lying on the water, or a nymph drifting helplessly in the current, then the ideal presentation would come to the fish with little or no current-induced drag.

On large trout streams being fished with the aid of a boat, raft, or float-tube, the downstream presentation is most easily and effectively accomplished by means of a technique called the Fall River Twitch. I will describe that method in detail in a moment, after surveying some of the other presentational possibilities of the pool. The Twitch is also possible to achieve on smaller pools from the bank or from a wading position upstream of feeding fish.

The fish may or may not be in a chasing mood. The best way to determine this is to start fishing at the head of the pool, quartering casts across the current using a mended, broadside drift of the fly that's allowed to sweep naturally across current and come to rest directly below the casting position. If this presentation is met quickly with a strike, then the same broadside delivery should be repeated until the pool has been thoroughly combed. If it does not meet with a response, then alternate casts should be allowed to sink deeply and stripped back towards the angler in an active recovery. The stripping retrieve is illustrated. The dead broadside drift is often the most

Pools often are among the most consistently prime locations for rainbows. Trout can detect movement well beyond the water when the pool's surface is slick.

effective when fishing with leech imitators, such as the Wooly Bugger. The stripping recovery usually prompts more strikes when fishing with streamer flies, like the Marabou Muddler, suggesting baitfish or immature trout.

The Fall River Twitch

Although the Fall River Twitch technique for delivering a floating or near-surface nymph fly without drag has been in use for decades, it is not a method well-understood by a majority of fly fishermen throughout the United States. Bud Lilly indicates that it probably evolved on Montana waters. I first encountered the technique on the Fall River in northern California, which is a very large, slow-flowing spring creek requiring the use of a boat to fish. And it was on the Fall River that professional flyfishing guide Carl Jaeger brought the technique to near-perfection.

Carl uses the Fall River Twitch to present dry flies and near-surface nymphs. A floating strike indicator is attached to the leader when fishing the nymph.

When fishing dry flies, Carl prefers to employ the method in the middle of a heavy hatch of mayflies or caddis. He

Rainbows found in large, smooth-surfaced pools like this one will frequently move in late in the day to feed upon forage fish and minnows. Gerlach prefers to fish shallow pools like this well after the sunlight is off the water, or prior to sunup. Note the "magic trout triangle" association with the riffle and run in the background.

watches for actively feeding trout before making any sort of presentation.

Once locating a pod of feeding rainbows, Jaeger positions up and slightly across stream from them. This gives him the flexibility to present the fly to the visibly feeding trout, or to any that may later start feeding directly downstream or across and down on the other side.

A very straight cast to the feeding lane of the trout is made so that the fly lands between four and ten feet upstream and slightly beyond the lane. As soon as the cast line is down on the water, the rod tip is raised to straighten the line and draw the fly into the precise center of the feeding lane.

With the line held firmly to the rod grip by the casting hand index or middle finger, three feet of line is stripped from the reel by the line hand, or taken from loose line peeled into the bottom of the boat prior to making the cast. This is pinched against the rod grip also, forming a three-foot-long loop of line.

The line loop held by the index finger of the casting hand is quickly fed through the guides by snapping the rod

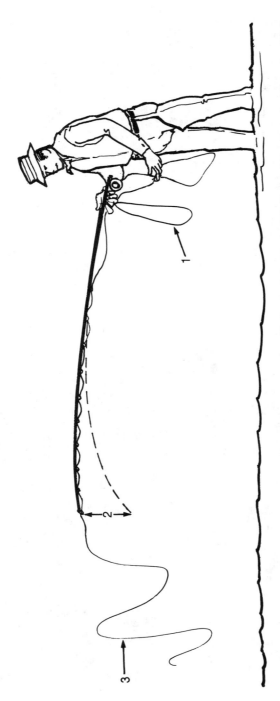

The Fall River Twitch. To perform this drag-free, downstream presentation: (1) Form a 3-foot loop of fly line, holding it against the grip with the index or middle finger of your casting hand. (2) Snap the rod tip up and down, releasing the loop so it shoots out the rod tip to form slack-line on the water. (3) Simultaneously with the release of the line-loop, another line-loop should be formed and held. This is repeated until the fly has drifted downstream to where you saw the fish rise.

Professional guide Carl Jaeger works out slack line onto the surface of the Fall River in California, during a spinner-fall.

The fly drifts only a few feet until a nice trout takes it in.

Jaeger carefully removes the barbless, size 16 cream/tan parachute dry fly from the trout's lip.

The rainbow is free to fight another day.

tip downwards. *Simultaneous* with this snapping of the loose line through the guides another three-foot line loop is being formed. The sequence is repeated to feed slack line—under control—as far downstream as needed. An entire fly line can be paid out this way and maintained under control to set the hook, although that is not necessarily recommended. Small trout can be bypassed, by adjusting the tension of the line to cause drag until the fly floats past them.

Frankly, it is the most deadly method of dry fly fishing and strike-indicator nymphing I've encountered in a lifetime of fly fishing. On smooth-running pools or meandering water, rig up a 15- to 20-foot tapered leader having a tippet at least three, preferably five feet long. Depending on current speed, obstructions in the water and the size of the rainbows, I normally fish the Twitch using a 5X or 6X tippet with size 14 to 18 dry flies.

The same technique has also proved useful to me when fishing for steelheads with much stouter tackle. It is sometimes the *only* effective way to work a steelhead bucktail downstream into a pocket behind a boulder. In this instance, the response to the slack-line offering is invariably a smashing strike.

The resident rainbow's taking of the dry fly or nymph fished on the Twitch is usually deliberate, characteristic of the rainbow's rise-form in the slow-moving currents of a spring creek. If one uses the method to fish for trout feeding in a riffle or run, a large corkie or a well-doped poly-yarn strike indicator helps a great deal in detecting the strikes. In those faster currents, however, some fish take in the fly and turn downstream, hooking themselves.

Meandering Water

The meander is very slow-moving water characteristic of meadow stretches of spring creeks, irrigation ditches, and slow-moving stretches of dam tailwaters. Like the pool, the meander's surface is relatively unruffled, except when a breeze is blowing. Because of the abundance and variety of natural trout foods normally found there, meanders also can be considered to be *consistent* rainbow feeding water.

Because of the abundant food, very large trout tend to home-base in meandering stretches. And, as in pools, one can expect the trout in meanders to be extremely wary when feeding actively on hatched insects, spinners, wind-blown hoppers, ants, beetles, and emerging nymphs or pupating caddis.

The stream bottom in the meander frequently tends to be weedy during the late spring, summer, and fall months. Winter ice-over conditions tend to knock down the weed growth in northerly climates. But when the weeds are trailing below the surface, or have grown all the way to the surface, presentations of flies and playing hooked trout are affected.

Virtually invisible variations in current speed occur across the breadth of most meanders. Oftentimes, this makes across-stream or up-and-across-stream dry fly presentations extremely difficult. Fly drag runs rampant. Mending the line may be only a partial solution to it. An upstream delivery from a boat or wading position tends to "line" and frighten feeding fish, particularly those which cannot be delivered with a Reach Cast that draws the line away from their fields of vision.

Meandering water is characteristic of spring creeks, such as the Fall River in California. In slow-moving reaches like this one bordered by reeds, damselfly and dragonfly hatches may occur. The ideal tactic would be to use a downstream delivery by means of the Fall River Twitch. Here the author prepares to fish, then lift anchor and reanchor at 2, 3, 4, and 5, where the boat in the distance is anchored. Since no rises are in evidence here, a strike-indicated nymph will be used, the casts "fanned" towards the reeds, as in a, b, c, and d. Presentations would be made directly to the fish, in the event of a rise.

When the weed growth in a meander is high, the downstream slack-line delivery may afford the better of the two options. This prevents the fly from becoming snagged on weeds as it otherwise might when cast up-and-across the current. It also delivers the fly directly into the trout's field of vision without the leader entering the trout's window before the fly. In my opinion, the Fall River Twitch and the Long-Tippet Technique are the best. The latter is credited to Bill Lawrence, former owner of Hot Creek Ranch in the eastern Sierras of California. Until the refinement of the Fall River Twitch, it was one of the few ways a *perfect,* drag-free float of a dry fly could be achieved in difficult, meandering water or eddies.

The objective of the cast is to achieve maximum slack in the tippet without sacrificing accuracy or fly control. For small- to medium-size streams, a 7-foot rod with a very soft tip is ideal. This is used with a 5-weight double-tapered fly line of the floating type.

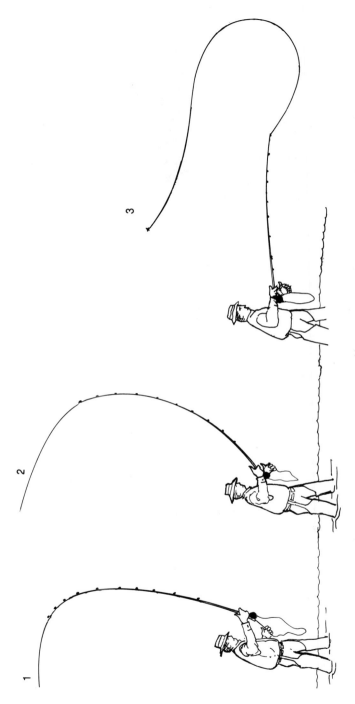

Long Tippet Casting Technique. The forward "kick" in the casting stroke (1 and 2) is delivered with a strong, fast wrist snap. This causes the line to flow out (3) in a configuration that will cause the long tippet to pile up when landing in the water.

current

The result should look something like this. Possible applications of the method are seen in the following three illustrations.

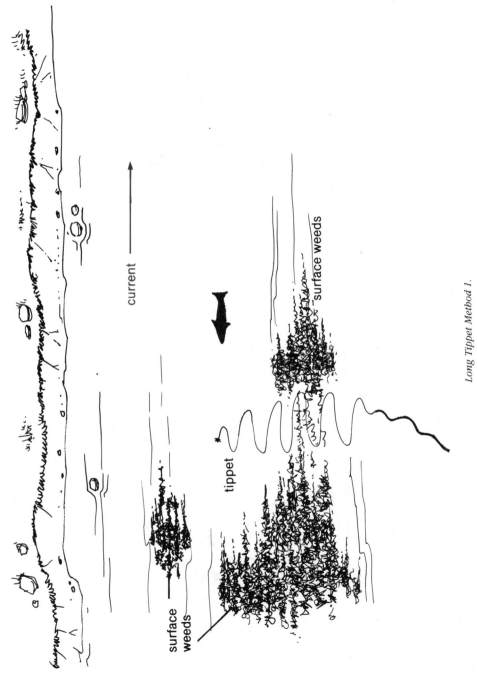

surface weeds

surface weeds

surface weeds

tippet

current

Long Tippet Method 1.

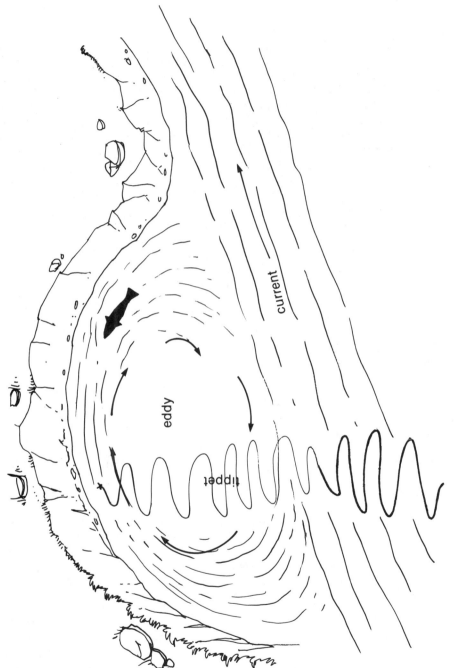

current

eddy

tippet

Long Tippet Method 2.

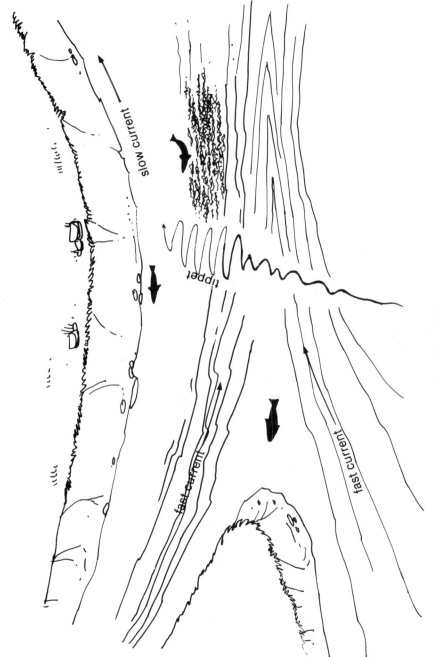

Long Tippet Method 3.

The leader is a 9-foot knotless taper with a .017-inch butt and .006- or .005-inch tippet. An additional 15 to 20 feet of the same tippet is attached to the basic leader. This arrangement is compatible with flies from size 16 to size 28.

It should be cautioned that using tippets longer than 15 feet makes it difficult to deliver the fly properly in a breeze or wind.

The forward "kick" in the casting stroke is delivered with a very fast, severe *wrist-snap* at about the ten o'clock position, if you're a right-handed caster. This causes the line to flow towards the target in a wave-like configuration, the leader tippet falling in a pile upon itself in the water. With practice, the angler can control the amount of slack thrown into the tippet. But by practice, I mean a lot of practice! It is an extremely difficult tactic to learn and to remain proficient. Precise timing is required. Perfectly designed and balanced tackle is essential.

On larger streams, an 8-foot, soft-tipped fly rod carrying a 7-weight line is more ideal. For this outfit, a 9-foot base-leader, tapering from .022 to .010 inch permits casting larger dry flies.

Leader butt size is critical. The terminal tackle used with a 5-weight line simply will not function correctly using a 7-weight line.

In learning the technique, the author suggests starting practice using an 8-foot tippet, then lengthening the tippet to 15 feet once some degree of proficiency is achieved. Practice should be done on the water.

As difficult as the Long-Tippet Method may be to learn, it can be employed along with the Fall River Twitch to double your success on large trout in eddies, meanders, and certain kinds of pools. It is well worth the effort, in my opinion.

The dry fly, however, is only one aspect of fishing the more productive meandering stream. Where mayfly and caddis hatches occur, opportunities will exist to catch the trout on both nymph and emerger flies. Some such streams also will have abundant freshwater shrimps, annelids and forage fish in meandering stretches. Where abundant weed growth is present near the surface and extending down into the mid-waters, fishing any of them on sink-tip or sinking lines can be extremely difficult, if not impossible.

Fishing the nymphs and emergers on directly upstream or downstream presentations in channels between weeds is one effective solution. If the trout are "chasing," then streamer flies cast quartering across the flow and retrieved quickly near the surface may provoke a smashing response.

In some, like the Bighorn river in Montana, masses of moss and pondweed tend to be broken loose from the river bottom when water is released from the dam upstream. This also interferes periodically with the use of sink-tip and full sinking lines.

Although no two spring creek or tailwater meanders fish exactly the same, in my experience, one behavioral tendency of the fish does seem to be common in many having abundant hatches throughout the season. The large trout seem to look up towards the surface much of the time.

David W. Corcoran, Gregg Lilly's partner in a great flyfishing store and guide service (The River's Edge) in Bozeman, Montana, has fished the fabled Bighorn river extensively. In discussing tailwater stream tactics with him, he singled out the upward-looking tendency of fish as the most *distinguishable* characteristic of the Bighorn fishery, which consists of both browns and rainbows.

On that river, he said, the floating fly line is the most useful, both because of the upward-looking trout and the masses of moss and pondweed sometimes adrift in the current.

Because the fish there tend to pod up in groups of as many as thirty trout, browns and rainbows feeding together in medium-speed runs of two to four feet in depth, upstream dry fly fishing and strike-indicator nymph fishing fre-

quently produce more hookups from a single pod of fish than a downstream, slack-line presentation.

The reason this is so when working very large pods of fish, says Corcoran, is that hooking the "lead" fish using the downstream delivery tends to spook other trout feeding in the same pod. Approaching the trout from the downstream direction permits quickly hustling hooked fish down and away from the balance of the feeding trout.

What prompts the Bighorn trout to so carefully scrutinize the near-surface waters are abundant hatches of mayflies, caddis, and stoneflies. There are also freshwater shrimps and a red-colored,

Frightfully wary trout and tight playing quarters prompted this angler to make upstream deliveries to nymphing trout on Silver Creek in Idaho.

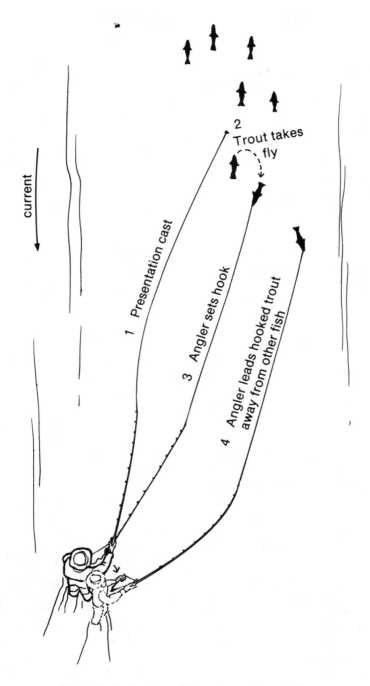

The tactical advantage of the upstream presentation.

aquatic annelid known locally as a "blood worm" in abundance. Yet, because of floating and submerged weed, the approach to fishing these seems to be best accomplished with the up- or up-and-across-stream delivery. There, says Corcoran, the strike-indicator may need to be placed as far as eight feet above the fly on the leader, depending on water depth. The majority of the spring creeks I've fished also tend to fish very well by this method, provided consistent hatches occur across the season to prompt the trout to keep their eyes on or near the surface.

When fishing the meander, however, the fly fisherman should be prepared to discard all the rules he may have learned previously about trout behavior. Each meander seems to have its own little quirks of trout feeding activity. One needs to be observant and willing to ask questions of local anglers to tune in on the specific patterns of feeding on these food-rich habitats.

Riffles

If one were to ask me where I might automatically start looking for rainbow trout in a stream with which I am totally unfamiliar, my answer would simply have to be in the riffles. This would be especially true during the time of year when maximum insect hatching activity takes place.

There are two reasons I feel this way. One, of course, relates to the rainbow's need for oxygenated water. The other is based on the rainbow's tendency to feed actively in a riffle throughout the times of day when insect hatches are underway.

I have the same good feelings about riffles when it comes to fishing for steelheads, but for different reasons. One of these relates to the aggressiveness steelheads often show towards a fly while they're occupying or traveling upstream through the riffles. The others are due to the attraction to the steelhead in summer offered by the well-oxygenated water, and the type of holds it affords them.

Riffles vary greatly from one to another. Each riffle must be assessed in terms of its depth and speed, and the particular kinds of trout or steelhead cover it may offer.

In fishing for resident rainbows, riffling water offers opportunities to fish variously with dry, wet, nymph, and streamer/bucktail flies. When trout cannot be directly observed feeding on hatching insects, the obvious tactical approaches are to fish with nymphs or wet flies.

Fishing effectively with nymphs or wets in riffles of wadeable depths has been most deadly for me when directed in an upstream manner. The short-line, high-sticking presentation of a nymph fished on a leaded leader beneath a strike indicator has provided consistently better results than other methods in my fishing.

This is not the case in steelhead fishing in deeper riffles where the across-and-downstream sweep of the fly has produced better results. I use a sink-tip, Wet Head, or sinking shooting-taper line to work a bucktail through the riffle, starting at the head of the riffle and probing the waters downstream. In summer-run fishing, I'll make between two and five casts from each wading position, then take a couple of shuffles downstream, repeating the process to the tail of the riffle. When winter-run fishing, my tactical

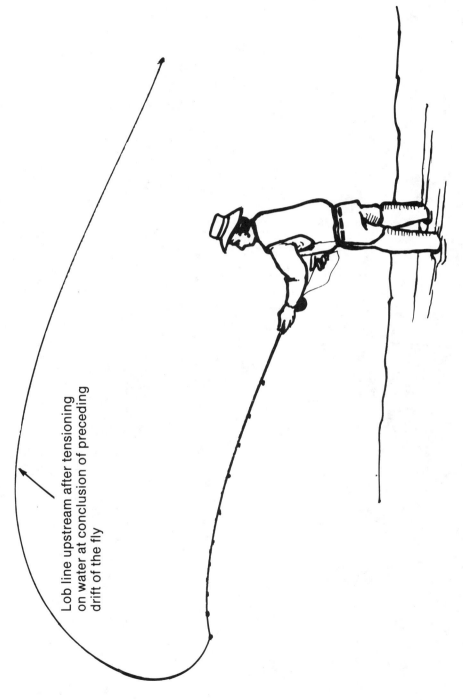

Lob line upstream after tensioning on water at conclusion of preceding drift of the fly

High-Sticking Technique. Twenty to thirty feet of line and leader are lob-cast up or up-and-across the current.

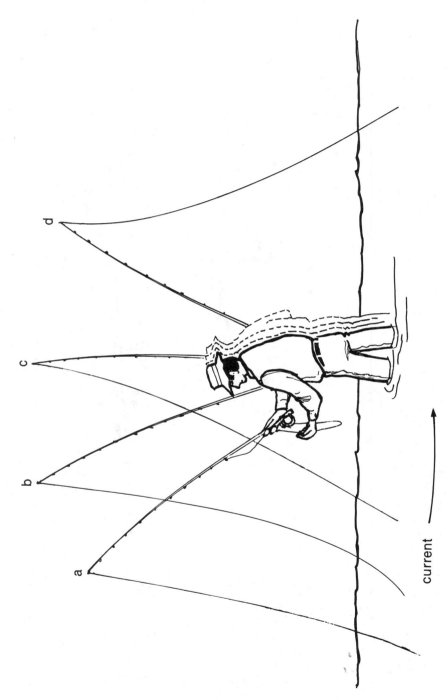

current →

As the fly drifts back towards the angler, the rod is raised increasingly higher to prevent excess slack from forming in the line (a, b, c). The line is allowed to swing past the angler and to straighten fully before the next cast is lobbed. Keep your eye on the strike indicator (d). If you see the slightest twitch or hesitation, set the hook. Repeat this type of cast as you slowly work your way upstream through the riffle.

Allan Rohrer "high-sticking" a nymph and strike indicator at the current edge leading from a run into a riffle.

approach to the riffle is more or less the same, only slower and more methodical. I may make as many as a dozen casts from a single position in the water.

If the riffle contains depressions and pockets likely to harbor *holding* fish, I will devote more attention to those lies, when fishing for rainbows and steel-heads.

Riffling water has upcurrents that tend to push a sunken fly towards the surface. I use the *shortest leader possible* when fishing riffles with sink-tip or sinking fly lines. Usually, this will be between two and five feet long. For the two-foot leader, I simply loop the leader to the

mono loop at the tip of my fly line. Instead of using a perfection loop knot on the tippet, I employ the stronger sur-geon's loop knot there. The mono loop on the tip of the fly line is made from about six inches of 15- or 20-pound-test monofilament internal nail knotted to the line's tip.

The same rig is used when fishing resident trout streams. In this case, I affix the tippet material directly to the line tip by means of an external nail knot. The reason for this is that I use finer leader material for rainbow fishing than for steelheading. The differences in diam-eter between the tippet and loop at-

Bud Lilly works the productive waters of a Madison River riffle with a dry caddis.

tached to the line are then excessive. This tends to fracture finer leader material when a fish strikes.

Dry fly fishing also is possible in riffling waters, both for rainbows and steelheads. A straight upstream or quartering up-and-across presentation provide short, effective drag-free floats of the fly.

One of the largest steelheads I ever lost was hooked following an up-and-across presentation of an Orange Optic steelhead fly into a deep riffle flowing into the pool below.

The object here was to bottom-bounce the Optic through the frothy zone where the riffle tumbled into the pool. And it certainly did work! The fly

stopped bouncing, cold, stone dead in the water. I'd lost a half-dozen Optics to the stream bottom that morning. So my immediate reaction was to rear back on the rod and exclaim: "Rats!" Then, I felt the rod tip bounce a couple of times. It was nearly yanked underwater as a heavy fish charged across the riffle and rolled to the surface, displaying a broad spotted tail and brick-red swath of color down its side.

The steelhead then raced into the base of the riffle and tore the surface in a series of lashing, twisting rolls and jumps! I put on the pressure and finally led the steelhead into the pool. It appeared to weigh in the neighborhood of

15 pounds, and, although obviously tiring, it had enough vitality left to make a powerful run deep into the pool. While doing this, my line became fouled on a large boulder and I lost both the steelhead and my shooting taper.

Runs

Runs are moderately-paced currents flowing over what may be a wide variety of river-bottom materials.

Runs having rocky or boulder-strewn bottoms tend to offer the best potential for rainbows, in my experience. Those having abundant aquatic food can be looked upon as consistent places for locating aggressively feeding rainbows. In steelhead rivers, the runs flowing several feet deep and having boulders on the bottom frequently are used as holding areas by steelheads needing a rest, provided they're located near the tops of long rapids.

Runs offer possibilities for several types of presentation, including the dry fly, nymphs, and streamers. The fly line selected for fishing the run depends on the type of fly being fished and on the depth and the speed of the current.

On trout streams having fairly shallow runs of slow to moderate speed, condi-

Bud Lilly works a flat spot in a riffle by starting to fish in relatively quiet water (1–7), then gradually fishing upstream, well into the broken water at the riffle's seam (8–12). He's dry fly fishing in this photo, but the approach would be similar using a nymph and strike indicator.

Because this run is relatively uniform between the angler and the current seam, an up-and-across dry fly presentation produced splendid results here.

tions may be ideal for either the Fall River Twitch presentation of the dry fly or strike-indicatored nymph. If the currents across the run are sufficiently uniform in speed, an up-and-across stream presentation may be equally effective.

Deep, rocky runs flowing through oxbow bends in the river are productive situations for presenting large nymphs and streamers using a broadside drift. The broadside drift is the ideal method of presentation, because fish may be lying practically anywhere waiting for food to drift into view.

Fast-flowing runs along straight shorelines tend to have fish lying in well-defined pockets. From a drift boat, these runs are most effectively fished by casting to within a couple of inches of the shoreline, then rapidly retrieving the fly using 3 or 4 stripping recoveries, to coax the fish into chasing it. This is a situation in which the floating line and heavily weighted fly are ideal, because of the need for repeated, rapid-fire deliveries and retrieves to hit likely pockets as they come into casting range.

Fishing similar water from a wading position permits more thorough water coverage by means of a weighted fly and a sink-tip line. Several probing casts can be directed to each pocket to assure any fish lying there will see the fly. To do this, a cast angled slightly down-and-

This oxbow bend held several rainbows the day Mark Daly and I fished it. The presentation used was a broadside drift, which ran the fly close to the shore where a well-defined seam and eddying pockets can be seen (a *and* b).

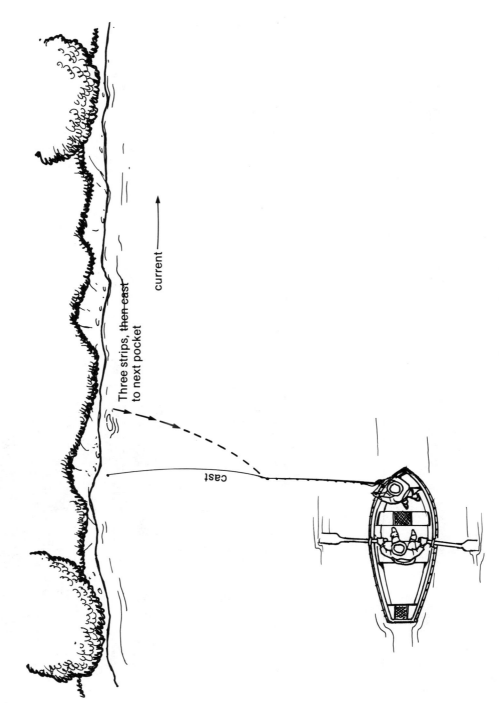

Three strips, then east
to next pocket

current →

cast

Fishing a heavily weighted fly to an undercut in a run.

A good run for fishing a heavily weighted Marabou Muddler on a Sink-Tip line. Fast strip-ins coaxed a trout into "chasing" the fly from its shady lie.

The narrow, deep slot against the rip-rapped bank in this steelhead run is best fished by means of a broadside drift, using a heavily weighted fly or a sink-tip line.

Although some of the steelhead traveling up this riffle-like run will follow the outer current edge, some will travel upstream within a few feet of the shore. A down-and-across-stream offering has the best chance of intercepting moving fish.

across the current allows both a natural sweep of the fly through the pocket and a stripping-in recovery. More hook-ups from strikes generally result.

The tactical approaches to steelhead runs are similar to those used on runs harboring resident rainbows. In the event the run is more or less compressed into a narrow main flow, then the broadside drift tends to keep the fly in front of the fish longer than a down-and-across delivery.

On the other hand, if the run has a breadth across which the fish may be distributed, the down-and-across delivery aimed at sweeping across current is more logical.

Reading the steelhead run involves both determining the nature of the river bottom and evaluating how the current is likely to affect the location of the fish. When the water is clear, of course, there may be sufficient visibility through the water to get an idea of the character of the river bottom where one wants to fish. When the water is off-color, a look at the shore-line rock formations leading into the water will sometimes provide a good feel for what the bottom will be like further into the river.

When steelheads are on the move, it may not be necessary to start fishing at the head of a run and work patiently down through it. Enough traveling fish

One look at the type of rock leading into this steelhead "traveling" water indicates two things. The run is extremely likely to hold steelheads when they are moving, and the wading will be tricky.

Steelheads were on the move when this fish was hooked on a dry fly near the large rock behind the angler.

Fenton Roskelley started fishing this drift as high as possible, using a down-and-across presentation.

100 yards downstream, Roskelley encounters broken, slower-moving water. Since this is steelhead "traveling" water, he seeks maximum water coverage, using long casts down-and-across.

may simply come to you to provide some action. But when the water is cold and the fish are holding, extremely thorough water coverage may be needed to locate the fish. My own strategy is to assume that all steelheads are "holding" steelheads, until they prove to my satisfaction they are on the move by rolling, or by coming to the fly at a location where I've just caught several fish. In other words, I *move* through the steelhead run, at least until I've discovered that is not necessary to catch fish.

To do this, I start fishing at the extreme upstream end of what appears to be the likely steelhead water. Then I make several casts, step downstream a few shuf-

fles and make several more casts. This is repeated until I've completely combed the run with my fly, whether it may be thirty feet long or a quarter-mile in length. If several fish are hooked as I course down through the run, I may be prompted to fish through it a second, or even third time.

If I happen to be fishing for summer-runs in relatively warm water, I may make a first pass through the run using a dry fly or riffling wet fly. A light hit from a fish may prompt me to change to a sink-tip or sinking shooting-taper line. When the water is below 50 degrees F., however, I always start fishing with some sort of sinking fly line, experimenting

The slick in this holding water between Fenton Roskelley and the partly submerged rock indicates a channel. This hot spot has produced more steelheads over the past thirty years than any other in the river. Roskelley thoroughly combs this pocket in the run.

"hot" spot

The upper part of the run tends to hold stacked steelheads early and late in the day. Methodical combing the water by sweeping, down-and-across presentations produces well here (1, 2, 3, 4,), and for some distance further downstream.

with various sink-rates until I hook bottom often enough to be certain the fly is running deeply.

One of the most important tactics in coaxing steelheads to the fly involves leaving the fly in the water well after it has swung across the current and come to rest below your casting position. Steelhead often follow a fly all the way across the run without taking. This tactic assumes that a steelhead has done just that, and that the fish may need a little coaxing to make a pass at the fly.

To coax the strike from a fish that has followed the fly in this way involves one of several ploys. One is to jiggle the fly with the rod tip, let it rest a moment, then jiggle and rest the fly a few additional times before preparing to cast

again. Another is to make a few quick strip-ins, then let the fly drift back to the resting position, repeating the tactic several times before making the next cast. Still another, which I use when fishing riffles tailing into slow-moving pools, involves slowly stripping in the fly as one might when fishing for trout in a similar pool.

All three of these tactics have produced fish for me. Over the years, the coaxing tactics have resulted in increasing my catch of steelheads by as much as twenty percent.

Rapids

Some rapids are the fastest-flowing, most turbulent waters of the stream or

Each of these locations is one in which traveling steelheads tend to hold. Here, the approach to the holding pockets is through a rather swift, shallow rapids, below which the fish tend to accumulate overnight. In this one, the hot spot is best reached from the 3 casting position, well out into the rapids.

This holding run is about 200 yards upstream from a short, swift rapids. Here, the fish probably hold only briefly before continuing upstream. Wading and water coverage are limited by deep water beyond casting position 3.

This third holding run is 400 yards upstream of a powerful, deep rapids. In this run, since there is a clearly defined current edge, the broadside presentation provides the best water coverage. The angler here can fish downstream another hundred yards or more.

river. But that does not mean one needs to view *all* rapids as being unfishable. Many contain pockets of slower-moving current ideal for rainbows to rest while migrating or to feed. When viewing rapids for their flyfishing possibilities, it is necessary to look upon them in a way that differentiates these fishable zones from those flowing too rapidly for a fish to swim comfortably or a fly to be run in an enticing manner.

Because rapids tend to be the most potentially dangerous areas of a river to fish, from a wading or boating standpoint, personal safety should always override any tactical fishing decisions. No fish is worth drowning or breaking bones. The initial tactical decision you should make is that only those stretches offering safe approaches will be considered. Most often these will be slower-moving edge-waters, well away from the dangerous flows in the main current.

These will often conceal some of the largest rainbows in the river.

Some of the more productive edge-waters resemble deep, rocky runs on small streams. Often they can be fished directly from the bank using an up-and-across delivery. Probe the closer waters first before directing casts further out along the current edge.

Large boulders may be scattered about in shallow, riffle-like rapids. Downstream from them, pool-like pockets may exist. Summer-run steelhead, in particular, tend to hold there when the river's dropping, or when the oxygen content of the

These look like dangerous rapids in which to fish. And they are. But rainbow trout feeding on eggs dropped by spawning salmon can be caught by fly fishing in locations such as 1, 2, 3, and 4 by fishing the shore-waters. Salmon-egg flies produce good results in this sort of situation.

rapids water may be higher than else-where in the stream. It is a kind of loca-tion where a floating fly line and a weighted fly hold an excellent chance of meeting an aggressive fish.

One such boulder-pocket comes to mind in particular. This huge black rock is about twenty-five yards from shore in

a rapids. The rapids is located but a short distance upstream from perhaps the fin-est traveling water for steelheads in the lower reaches of my favorite summer-run stream.

The main tactical problem in fishing the pocket is that the stretch is adjacent to a state fish and game department

Pockets of highly flyfishable water exist in most rapids. In this one, the angler is presenting a dry fly in a downstream direction.

In tumbling, mountain streams, like this one, most of the better-sized rainbows will be found in little pools. An upstream approach is virtually mandatory to avoid frightening the trout. When approaching them, watch out for where your shadow falls.

camping area and parking lot. When weekending fly fishers see a steelhead caught from behind that boulder, they are certain to compete for fishing time behind that rock.

Knowing this to be the case, my strategy is to fish the pocket only very early in the morning, well before campers are up and about, or when the campsite is empty of anglers. And since the best time of day to fish the pocket tends to be between 9:30 a.m. and 2:00 p.m., when fish moving up into the rapids have stopped to rest, my strategy normally is to fish there only on weekdays when there is less chance of my being ob-

served catching a trout. This takes a great deal of self-control, to be sure, but it's worth it. Another difficulty in fishing the pocket is that it is surrounded by powerful currents. A straight-across or up-and-across presentation tends to race the fly too rapidly through the pocket for a fish to respond. Because of this, I approach the pocket from directly downstream and proffer the fly nearly directly upstream.

On several occasions, however, I have approached the pocket from well upstream and run a bucktail down through the current seam using a Fall River Twitch-type release of slack line. This presentation has resulted in over a half-dozen steelheads.

Perhaps the most productive of all the different kinds of rapids for rainbows and steelheads are canyon stretches comprised of cataracting currents formed by large boulders on the river bottom. Inexperienced anglers tend to avoid these stretches, because they frequently appear to be unfishable or beyond their skills at wading and casting. From a casting standpoint at least, this is not true. The pools below the cataracts are extremely easy to fish using the downstream twitch or upstream high-sticking presentation of a dry fly or nymph.

Wading these stretches to fish is another matter. If the rocks are the least bit slippery, it requires the use of a stout wading staff, aluminum creepers, and very good balance. The wading is potentially dangerous. Fishing these stretches is a questionable practice for anyone not in top physical condition. It's darned hard work! Tom Stouffer and I discovered a pod of steelheads holding in this sort of lie. It was in a deep canyon stretch, aglow with leaves turning yellow and amber in the fall, the air fresh and sweet-smelling from the surrounding conifer forests. The river cataracted into golden pools of clear water over granite boulders, some as large as an auto.

Directly below where I stood drinking in the beauty of the scene from a high bank lay a four-foot deep pool some thirty feet wide and fifty feet long. The bottom of the pool consisted of pulverized granitic gravel and sand.

The bright sunlight reflecting off the great slabs of granite around me hurt my eyes, so I flipped down my Polaroid clip-ons. That was better. Again I scanned the snow-capped mountains in the distance, then glanced back down into the pool.

This time the surface glare off the water was virtually gone, due to the polarized sunglasses. What I saw caused me to catch my breath! Five gorgeous steelheads lay finning quietly in the pool.

I hailed Tommy and asked him to join me; to move near with caution so as not to frighten the fish. We stood there for several moments, saying nothing, wondering what to do next.

At that time, he was recovering from surgery following a serious injury sustained in Viet Nam. He was not in any condition to scramble down the steep bank and make a try for the fish. I was, but a quick look downstream showed a near endless stretch of cataracts falling away like gigantic stair steps. What would one do if a fish were hooked and turned tail downstream? Though these fish did not appear to be large, as steelheads go, possibly five to eight pounds, a determined downstream rush by any of them was certain to result in a broken tippet. The gigantic granite boulders prevented any possible following of a hooked fish.

I decided to give it a try anyway. Losing a running steelhead in an impossible situation was nothing new to me. So I rigged my Fenwick FF-112 fly rod with a line and tied on a size 4 Skunk bucktail. This I knotted to a tippet testing 10 pounds. I had selected the strong, fiberglass fly rod, because my intention was to *hold* any hooked fish in that small pool, regardless of the consequences.

Tommy and I figured that I'd only be able to achieve a downstream presentation of the fly once or twice without spooking the trout in the clear water. So we decided that he'd remain high above the water and quickly indicate if the fly I cast was going to run to the fish or not. This would very definitely have to be a two-man effort.

I crept very slowly down the rockfall leading to the river's edge, using some willows to shield my movements. I kept my silhouette broken by willows, even while casting. Good grief! Those fish were less than twenty feet from where I stood!

Tom stood seventy-five feet above and back from me, a pair of binoculars riveted to the upper end of the pool. I made the first cast and snapped out three feet of slack line.

"Can you see the fly?" I shouted!

"Yep," said Tom. "Pull it back fast. Make the next cast three feet farther out."

I did that and again shouted: "Can you see the fly?"

"Yep," said Tom. "Wait a minute," he stammered as I continued to pay out slack line. "I can't see the fly anymore. A fish moved to it. Quick! Set the hook!"

I'd felt nothing, but reared back on the powerful rod. The pool blew up in my face! I'd hooked one of the larger female steelhead in the pod.

The steelhead dashed across the pool, shook its head and rolled. Then it raced for the down stream lip of the pocket and jumped, landing less than a yard from certain disaster. My heart sank. But I reared back and practically doubled-up the rod against the unyielding weight of the steelhead. The fished slashed across the pool again and jumped twice more, then jumped again! My heart was in my throat!

"Watch it! She's heading for the lip again!" yelped Tom. I reared back on the pounding rod tip and brought the fish to the surface in a slashing roll.

This went on for another five minutes. The steelhead eventually exhausted itself by jumping and pulling against the relentless pressure of the taut line. I was in an emotional shambles by the time I lipped the fish and removed the fly from its mouth. I cradled the beautiful trout in slack water for a full five minutes, until it had sufficiently recovered to swim from my hands.

It was undoubtedly the most exciting tussle I've had with a steelhead of any size. And it gave me great pleasure to release the trout to fulfill its destiny.

As I prepared to take down the rod so we could continue to another location, I started to clip the fly from the tippet. But that wasn't necessary. It parted easily between my fingertips. It had become so frayed in passing over rocks that one more determined wiggle by the steelhead would have caused it to part.

Although the tactical lessons derived from this experience require no further comment, they tend to lead naturally to an examination of how one should view rainbow trout water with an eye to playing and landing hooked fish.

Playing the Fish

Previewing a stretch as to how one might play fish hooked there can be a very important aspect of the rainbow fishing strategy. My way of approaching it is to eye the water downstream and upstream of where I intend to fish to determine both the ease of egress from the water and limitations as to how far I might be able to follow a large, hooked trout downstream. At the same time, I also try to identify any possible entanglements to the line that might interfere with my ability to bring the trout to where I stand in the water or lead it to the beach.

In spring creeks, weed growth poses a constant threat. The rainbow's speed and determination compound the threat. For once a rainbow has found that running and jumping are of no avail, like the brown trout, it will frequently try to dislodge the fly on some stream-bottom obstruction. Allowing the fish to do this risks immediate entanglement in the weeds. The rainbow's great speed allows even small fish in the 10- to 12-inch class to escape in that manner.

The obvious, logical solution to the problem should be to simply force the fish to swim head-up as it fights. Sometimes this can be done by lifting the rod high overhead in the same manner as when fighting a running bonefish over a shallow bottom to prevent coral from cutting the leader. Unfortunately, this doesn't usually work out as well when playing a heavy rainbow trout on a tippet testing as light as a pound or two. The slightest miscalculation in how much stress the tippet will bear practically always results in a break-off.

Similarly, the bass fisherman's tactic of intentionally letting the fish become entangled in the weeds, then reaching into the weeds to extract both bass and weeds is equally ineffective with fine tippets and heavy trout. The struggling of the heavy fish amongst the weeds often breaks the tippet.

Likewise, the tactic of throwing a long length of slack into the line to pressure the fish from downstream and, thus, cause it to turn upstream has little to offer. In a weedy stream, this may simply serve to entangle the downstream loop of line in additional weed.

About the only tactic I've found practical is to begin fishing this sort of water with an attitude in which I am willing to take a great deal of risk. As I step into the water, I say to myself: "OK. If you hook a fish, the *first* thing you're going to try to do before it runs is lift it towards the surface and quash its will to run. From the hookset, you—Gerlach old fellow—will take charge! If the leader parts, so be it!"

If the fish happens to be a relatively small trout, lifting the rod high above the head and simultaneously taking up the slack line by quickly stripping or reeling in turns the trick. But when the rainbow is a pound or more in weight, the odds of forcing it to turn upstream instead of downstream drop to less than fifty–fifty. Have no doubt about the likelihood of a break-off if the fish refuses to turn and you are rigged with fine tippet!

When the fish is unyielding, the flyfisher needs to be ready to let it run and jump, then reapply the maximum pressure before the trout has time to dive into the weeds. If the tippet survives this a couple of times, chances are the trout will be whipped. On rocky, freestone streams, the tactic isn't as necessary. Unless there are a lot of roots or downed trees in the water, letting the trout fight freely may be the most suitable tactic.

If it is your intent to release the fish unharmed, there is a better chance of its survival if you hustle it in as quickly as possible. A trout played until it's lying spent has far less chance of surviving than one forced to *come* while still struggling actively.

Rainbows of good size hooked in long runs or riffles frequently can be pressured into swimming into the shallows where they can be released with little harm. Steelheads of small size can be hustled as well, provided you let them have their heads for those first jumps and long runs. The trick here is applying maximum rod pressure on the fish when it is moving in your direction, or holding in the current.

Moving to a position slightly downstream of the fish to apply the pressure tends to further shorten the fight. This forces the fish to do one of two things, both of which are to *your* advantage. If the fish runs opposite to the direction of the pull, it is forced to expend more energy to battle both the pull from the rod and the force of the current. If it turns downstream, one can often gain a great deal of line and work the fish closer to the beach.

When the steelhead or rainbow has already expended much energy during its initial runs and jumps, relentless rod pressure when it is not running tends to further break its will to fight. It's a tactic learned in fighting tarpon and other saltwater species that applies equally well to rainbow trout in fresh water.

The reader should be cautioned that playing a rainbow or steelhead on a tight leash involves more risk of a break-off than a more cautious handling of the fish. I happen to be one of those willing to take the risk. You may not be.

7

Stillwater Tactics

A biologist friend had tipped me off to a privately owned 30-acre pond containing rainbow trout as large as four pounds. The state had acquired tenuous public access to it, provided littering would be controlled. Because the access had been acquired after printing the sport-fishing regulations for that season, the pond was likely to draw little attention until the following year.

My friend had agreed to disclose the location on the proviso I wouldn't jeopardize the access agreement. My writing an article about the place might attract a horde of anglers. The following season, flyfishing only regulations would apply, thus limiting use to some extent.

I decided to scout the pond on a sunny May morning. Since I was still weak from a bout with the flu, I left the car-top boat and float tube at home. I didn't feel quite up to the exertion of using either.

So I grabbed my flyfishing vest, checked the pockets to assure a selection of nymph and dry flies were there, and tucked a reel with extra spools of floating, sink-tip, and fast-sinking fly lines in the back-pouch. One rod would suffice, I figured, so I tossed that and a pair of wide-field binoculars into the back seat. I might need the binoculars to survey the more distant parts of the lake. A hike around the lake was out of the question in my weakened condition. Hip boots worn to fish the shallows near the access would have to suffice.

Upon arriving at the pond, I discovered that it was located in a delightful, pastoral setting. The water was very clear and extensive weed growth covered the bottom. From the road above,

Reedy areas of lakes frequently harbor abundant damselfly and dragonfly nymph populations. Here, Allan Rohrer uses a float tube to approach the weedy shallows of a flowage lake. He's fishing with a sink-tip line to achieve a "rising" return of the fly. Accompanying sketches show: the same tactic from a boat, detail of rising fly.

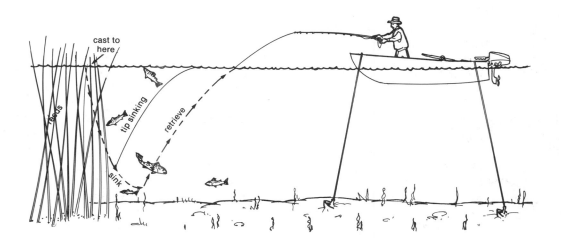

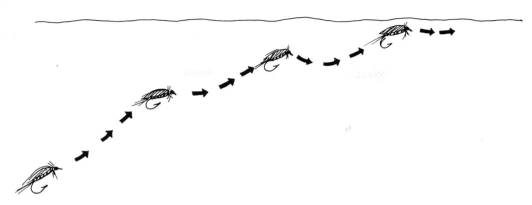

the water appeared to be no deeper than fifteen or twenty feet. A reedy island lay in the middle. On this lay remnants of a long unused duck blind. Numerous trout swirled in the shoreline shallows. Other fish rose head-and-tail in mid-pond.

I walked down the hill to the water's edge, carrying my fly rod rigged with a sink-tip line. The swirls of the trout feeding closest to shore indicated they were nymphing.

Once at the water's edge, it was apparent the trout were feeding on damselfly nymphs. The water was full of them. Others were hatching on reeds or flitting about in blue splendor. A spinner-fall also was in progress, possibly accounting for the mid-pond feeding activity.

I had attached a nine-foot leader tapering to 5X to the sink-tip line. To the tippet I knotted a size 10, 3XL Heather Nymph, which my friend Fenton Roskelley had designed to suggest damselfly nymphs.

The water dropped away quickly from the shoreline. I made an exploratory cast of seventy feet and let the fly sink to a count of "ten." Then, I began a slow, irregular hand twist recovery. The leader was almost back to the rod tip when I felt a "tick" at the fly and set the hook. A brightly colored 15-inch rainbow shot into the air, my lightly tinseled fly sparkling in its lip!

Releasing that fish, I made several more casts and retrieves before hooking another fish, this a 12-incher. Shortly after releasing that fish, my fly felt like it had grabbed a heavy weed-mass. I pulled on the line. A fish pulled back, this one a much heavier trout that zipped 100 feet of line from the reel, then jumped. From the look of it, the trout might have been one of the four-pounders my biologist friend had mentioned. It threw the fly on a second jump.

All this excitement had left my flu-wracked body shaky and perspiring. I returned to the car and left. But I was certain to return again.

What the incident represents, of course, is how the tactical approach works in a real-life situation. Although the fishing on that pond was exceptional, because of light fishing pressure, it is not atypical of the sort of action to be had elsewhere when the trout are feeding actively in the spring. The tactics flow directly from the conditions being met.

In this chapter, I'll come at them in much the same way I did for stream and river fishing, beginning with tackle.

Tackle

The need to variously probe lake depths from the surface to below thirty feet requires a considerable range of floating, sink-tip, and full-sinking fly lines. Also influencing tackle selection are windy conditions occurring frequently on lakes and how one intends to approach the water by wading, tubing, or from a boat.

Rods

Both the prevailing wind conditions and the distance one might need to cast affect rod selection for lake fishing. Shallow parts of lakes and ponds ranging down to about 20 feet can be probed very effectively using 5-, 6-, or 7-weight lines. Deeper areas, or when fishing in strong winds, are better met with the use of 7-, 8-, and sometimes 9-weight lines and the more powerful rods suitable for casting them.

Perhaps the best "compromise" line-weight is seven. This, matched with an 8½- or 9-foot rod permits the making of very long casts, yet reasonably delicate close-in presentations. The long casts permit making the long, underwater retrieves needed to keep flies in front of fish in deeper waters.

The ability to cope with wind also is important in a lake rod. In a head- or cross-wind, it is far more difficult to

Here Tommy Stouffer lays out a long cast to a rising fish in the pond.

achieve turn-over and directional control with a 5-weight line than it is with a 7-weight or heavier. Nine- and 10-weight balanced rods are most suitable for lake fishing with lead-core shooting tapers, or factory-made Deep Water Express or Cannonball fly lines.

Although rod length and action tend to relate more to your casting skill and preferences, those between eight and nine feet in length have proved to be the most suitable for my lake fishing. Nine- and even 9½-foot fly rods tend to be the ideal for float-tubing. For they allow longer, higher backcasts from a position low in the water. The 8- to 9-foot fly rods are altogether adequate for fishing from a boat.

Reels

What was said in the chapter on stream tactics regarding the need for a smooth-running drag system is equally important in lake fly fishing for rainbows. The same reels used for stream fishing are equally suitable, provided they'll handle the fly line and 50 to 100 yards of 20-pound-test backing line. Fishing for outsized Kamloops rainbows may require up to 200 yards of backing line, when the fish may run into the ten-pound-plus class.

Good reels for the general run of lake fly fishing include the Pfleuger model 1495½, the Scientific Anglers System 2 (lightweight model 7/8), and the Orvis Presentation model EXR IV.

Fly Lines

Having an adequate selection of fly lines with different sink-rates is quite essential to productive lake fly fishing.

Floating lines and sink-tips in two sink-rates also are needed to meet the variety of conditions encountered.

The floating lines will be used for fishing dry flies, emergers, and nymphs, as well as streamer flies in the extreme shallows. Floating lines and weighted flies, and sink-tip lines help achieve retrieves causing the fly to "swim" towards the lake's surface. The fast-sinking sink-tips are most useful in water depths ranging from five to ten feet. Extra-fast-sinking sink-tips extend the fishable depth to from fifteen to twenty feet. Their most applicable uses are over weedy food shelves during damselfly, caddisfly, and mayfly emergences.

Full-length sinking fly lines are the "big guns" in the lake fly fisher's arsenal. In most regions of the U.S. and Canada, fully eighty percent of the better lake fly fishing possibilities lie beneath the surface of the water. These lines used with short leaders let you get the fly down fast and work it very close to the top of the weeds or lake bottom.

Flies suggesting minnows, leeches, scuds, and nymphs all can be worked effectively on the full-length sinking fly lines. They are available in slow, fast-sinking, and extra-fast-sinking types, as well as in an intermediate type that can be greased to float if need be. I carry three sink-rates of sinking fly lines when I am venturing to unfamiliar waters. It makes a lot of sense to carry several sink-rates of sinking fly lines when one has no idea of the water depths that might be encountered.

Leaders

As in stream fishing, leaders for lake fly fishing should be scaled to the clarity of the water, the size and weight of the fly being used, and to how one wants the fly to behave in the water during retrieval.

The diameter of the tippet affects not only the ability to achieve a proper turnover of the leader when casting a certain weight of fly, but also the fly's *mobility* when being retrieved. In fishing nymphs and streamers under the surface, fine, limp tippets allow imparting more "wiggle."

For most lake fly fishing, leaders ranging between nine and fifteen feet provide adequate separation of line from fly to bring about strikes from rainbows. Except in unusual circumstances, tippets longer than three feet are not recommended. Tippets longer than three feet are difficult to straighten out when casting in windy or breezy conditions. Tippets from 6X to 3X will serve most dry fly fishing needs on lakes. Because the new copolymer monofilaments tend to be stronger for their diameters than conventional monos, I now tend to carry along 7X leader in addition to the other sizes.

Leaders longer than 7½ feet rarely are needed for deep-water nymph and streamer fly fishing. When the intent is to fish the fly very close to the lake bottom, three- to six-foot leaders eliminate the need to heavily weight the flies or add shot to the leader.

At depths where one can't see what lies on or near the bottom, and where the trout may average quite good size, a range of stronger tippets from 4X to 0X may be needed, in addition to the lighter ones carried for dry fly and near-surface nymphing.

Some fly fishers prefer to deploy leaders treated to sink rather than short leaders made from untreated monofilament. They reason that the leader treated to sink at the same rate as the fly line tends to eliminate much of the "line belly" occuring in untreated mono leaders. Some feel this makes it easier not only to feel light takes by trout, but also to straighten the leader/line combination in setting the hook.

Most fly shops carry a selection of both types of leaders, sinking and untreated. Harry Kime, a California fly fisher most noted for his saltwater fly-fishing adventures, long ago tipped me off to a good trick in preparing one's own sinking leaders. What it consists of is preparing a mixture of well thinned-down Pliobond cement and powdered graphite lead. This is then brushed onto the leader while it is stretched between a couple of nails. Several coats are applied, until the leader is thoroughly coated with the graphite/Pliobond mixture. The tippet, usually two or three feet long, is left uncoated. Factory-made coated leaders also are available in the braided-butt type. I use methyl-ethyl-ketone to thin the Pliobond. However, its vapors are potentially hazardous to your health. For that reason, it's a good idea to mix the stuff outside in the fresh air and apply it in a well-ventilated area where the vapors are not being inhaled by self, family, friends, or pets. The availability of the Sue Burgess sinking leaders practically eliminates the need for the mess or hazards of homemade ones.

Multiple Rigged Rods

One of the greatest contributors to improving your success ratio on rainbows in lakes involves being ready at all times to take advantage of fleeting opportunities. These include the trout suddenly pushing forage fish against the shoreline, or the emergence of a hatch of short duration.

When a small boat is being used as the on-water conveyance, this can be assured by keeping two or three fly rods rigged and ready at all times. On the relatively shallow lakes I prefer to fish, this means having separate fly rods rigged with floating, sink-tip, and fast-sinking lines at hand. On some lakes that I've fished, such as small flowages averaging less than ten feet deep, a dry fly outfit and a sink-tip might be all that would be required to meet the fishing possibilities. Having the fully-rigged outfits ready at hand lets you take full advantage of quickly developing opportunities without wasting time to change lines.

Obviously, carrying several rigged rods around on a float tube is not practical. In that fishing, carrying extra spools of line in the tube's storage pocket at least gives you the option of changing tactics. The same thing applies to lakes where you might want to wade an extensive length of shoreline. Extra spools of line tucked into the back pouch of a fly vest prevents the possibility of getting caught with only a sinking line in the middle of a fast-developing insect emergence or spinner fall. I cannot over stress the importance of having a reasonable selection of fly lines on hand at all times when lake fishing.

Fly Line Tapers

Lake fishing very often is a long-casting exercise in the wind. Because it is, I can't recommend double-taper fly lines as serious tools for lake fly fishermen. Although double-taper fly lines are ideally suited to fishing small to mid-sized streams in calm air, their limitations in distance casting practically eliminate them from serious consideration for lake, pond, or large-stream angling. Since even the lighter weight-forward fly lines can be rigged and adjusted to present flies delicately in small streams, I can very honestly admit that I see no benefit in including double-taper lines in my kit. The half-dozen double-tapers I own in light-line sizes haven't been out of the plastic storage bag in my garage for years. I don't bother with them anymore. There is nothing I can do with a double-taper fly line that can't be done as well or better with a well-designed weight-forward or triangle-taper. And that includes roll-casting. In my opinion, the double-taper line's main benefit lies in nostalgic traditionalism. For those to whom traditionalism may be more important than hooking trout feeding "way out" in a wind-riffle, I guess they serve a purpose.

Flies for Lake Fishing

When selecting flies for lake fishing, it's important to recognize that, in lakes, the angler has to impart most of the fish-attracting "wiggle." Additionally, a fly viewed by a trout in a lake is more clearly defined to the trout than one being tumbled along by the current. As a result, lake-inhabiting rainbows have a better chance to carefully inspect the fly and detect our fakery than stream trout.

My own experiences indicate that dry flies dressed in the relatively bushy "fast-water" style tend to be less effective on lakes than those tied in the sparse or no-hackle styles. Because the dry fly floating on the lake is rarely subject to being swept beneath the surface by current turbulence, adequate buoyancy is achieved by using minimal hackle, or none at all, as in the no hackle and Paradun ties. The fly's buoyancy in these comes from buoyant body and winging materials, such as polypropylene and deer or elk hair.

In lake flies for fishing beneath the surface, *mobility* of the leg and winging materials is important. The reason it is, is that active movement of those fly parts should result from even the most subtle hand-twist retrievals. This material softness also is important, because rainbows tend to hold onto soft-feeling nymphs and streamers longer than they do harder, stiffer, more rigid ones.

This is true even of flies representing relatively hard-bodied naturals, such as crayfish, snails and scuds. Even in these, artificials dressed from soft dubbings of muskrat, beaver, or polypropylene tend to outperform those incorporating more rigid materials.

Marabou feathers are a prime ingredient of the most effective lake flies suggesting leeches and forage fishes. In the case of the leech-imitators, it helps the angler simulate the undulating movements of the natural in the water. The Wooly Bugger pattern is one of the better ones.

In tying lake flies with marabou wings in styles suggesting forage fish, the angler-tyer should remember that the long, marabou wings tend to wrap around the bend of the hook when fishing if a less flexible underwing of bucktail or squirrel tail hairs is not applied. The Marabou Muddler fly pattern, one of the author's favorites, is a good example of how this underwing has been incorporated into a deadly combination of marabou, squirrel tail hairs, and tinsel chenille.

Terminal Rigging

Because of the lack of significant current in most lake areas, terminal rigging should enhance the mobility of the fly, rather than restrict it in any way. Although one might prefer the castability of hard monofilament leaders, their use should be restricted to the base-leader, not the tippet, when rigging for underwater fishing with wet flies, nymphs, and streamers. A more pliant material used for the tippet will enhance any action you impart to the fly by means of a retrieve.

Both knotted and knotless tapered leaders are suitable for lake fly fishing. As in stream fishing, the knotless tapered leaders tend to pick up less weed than knotted ones.

Although special riggings such as some described in the chapter on stream tactics may be used for certain lake situations, like inlet flows, for the most part, straight-forward tapered leaders in various lengths will suffice.

The strike indicator can be used on lakes to help detect otherwise imperceptible takes by trout of Chironomid emerger flies. And it can be used to do this from near the surface to as deeply as ten or fifteen feet.

The most effective Chironomid emerger or larva tactic is essentially a "do nothing" retrieve, that is to say, no retrieve at all. The cast is made so as to fully extend the fly line and leader onto the water. Only the natural movement of the lake water is relied upon to impart

Chironomid emerger patterns, such as this, often produce more strikes when fished with a "do nothing" retrieve.

gentle action to the fly. The reason for this presentation is simply that Chironomid larvae, pupae, and adults scarcely move in a perceptible way while in or on the water. Stripping or hand-twist retrieves tend to "turn off" the rainbows when they're working on the Chironomids.

A poly-yarn strike indicator affixed at the juncture of the tippet with the tapered leader provides a better chance of seeing the subtle twitches of the leader indicating underwater takes by the rainbows. When the fish are feeding deeply on Chironomids, first anchor the boat or float tube and *precisely* measure the depth of the water being fished. Cut a tippet an inch or two shorter than the depth of the water and permit the fly to sink very slowly without significant weighting. Very little movement by the trout mouthing the fly is needed to make

A "dead-still" lake surface like this requires a cautious, low-profile approach, such as being achieved by Allan Rohrer in his float tube.

the feather-light poly-yarn strike indicator twitch perceptibly.

Tactics for Lake Cover

Cover in lakes serves several needs of the rainbows. *Depth* and *shade* tend to be used more when escaping excessive warmth and when the trout are not actively cruising the shallows in search of food. *Turbulence* and *turbidity* frequently are used by rainbows to conceal themselves from forage fish, as are submerged *brush* and *trees.* The current and clarity edges associated with turbulence and off-color water thus can be looked upon as prime lake feeding locations where forage fish constitute a major source of trout food.

In lakes where the trout's food consists mainly of shrimps, snails, and aquatic insect life, the weedy food-shelf tends to be the prime feeding location.

Flyfishing tactics for lakes involve coping with both water textures and types of cover harboring food for the fish. The techniques used to fish the still portions of the lake are rather like those used to coax trout from backwater areas. Those needed to fish inlet streams are similar to methods that prompt the trout to strike in slow-moving meanders. The remainder of this chapter takes a look at the tactics for fishing the different kinds of lake cover and water texture. In their ascending order of difficulty to fish with flies, these include weedy shallows, drop-offs, submerged brush and timber, submerged points of land and humps, shoreline brush, gravel spawning shoals, inlets, outlets, underwater rock cliffs, and wind-riffles. While studying these tactics, the reader should be constantly reminded that these primes often are closely associated with one another. As a result, the tactics may have to be adjusted to suit the combination of differing conditions, rather than to a single set of circumstances.

Weedy Shallows

Weedy shallows can be looked upon as parts of the food shelf extending into no more than 20 or 30 feet of water. They constitute some of the most *consistent* primes in lakes harboring rainbow trout.

The weeds contain abundant aquatic life. Rainbows are almost certain to be feeding there whenever water temperature and pH levels permit. In northern-tier states, this will be from shortly after ice-out through late spring, then again in the fall as water temperatures in the shallows cool. In areas not affected by ice-over conditions, the weedy shallows may constitute rainbow feeding primes anytime of the year.

The prime trout-feeding time in weedy shallows is normally in the spring after the trout have come off the spawning gravel and the water temperature approaches 56 degrees F. The trout are "starved" after their exhausting spawn-

ing efforts. An abundance of insect life is on the move and hatching. This combination of hungry trout and abundant food tends to produce the fastest fly fishing of the year in the shallows.

There are countless opportunities for meeting massive hatches of mayflies, damselflies, dragonflies, and mosquitos. Ant mating flights take place. Crayfish are crawling from their winter burrows back towards rocky habitats. Snails and shrimps may abound.

Although dry fly fishing opportunities are numerous, the rainbows will accept nymph, leech, and shrimp patterns throughout the day, fair weather or foul. Some of the fastest fishing may occur on heavily overcast, rainy days lacking thunderstorm activity. Thunder and lightning normally put the lake rainbows off their feed for several hours.

Tactical approaches to weedy shallows include wading, float-tubing, and casting or trolling from a boat. When the lake-bottom is heavily matted with pond-weed or comprised of a thick layer of soft mud, wading is impractical, sometimes dangerous.

Float-tubing offers excellent presentational possibilities, provided the water is deep enough and the weeds do not extend so high in the water as to entangle the angler's feet.

My own preference is a small boat, such as a pram or a high-performance aluminum bass boat having a shallow-draft and sufficient stability to serve as a stand-up casting platform. Either oars or a quiet-running electric trolling motor are needed to maneuver the boat amongst the weed growth in shallow water.

Depending upon the character of the feed available, rainbow trout are likely to be found in weedy cover from the shore-line to over twenty feet of depth.

In deeper water, from eight to twenty feet, a good way to locate a pod of rainbows is to cast out a nymph on a sinking fly line and troll it along until a fish strikes. The boat is then anchored at the bow and stern so that a very straight, underwater retrieve can be accomplished by stripping or hand-twisting methods. If the action slows where the boat is anchored, the boat is then moved and re-anchored in a different location after locating fish by mooch-troll.

The sink-rate of the sinking fly line selected for the area being fished should be scaled to the depth of water. My own rule of thumb for sinking line selection is:

• 15 to 30 foot depth: extra-fast-sinking line (Hi-D)

• 8 to 15 foot depth: fast-sinking line

• 2 to 8 foot depth: slow-sinking or intermediate line

In the event that I opt to use a sink-tip line, then my choices are:

• 8 to 15 foot depth: extra-fast-sinking sink-tip line

• 2 to 8 foot depth: fast-sinking sink-tip line

When fishing nymph and streamer flies using sinking or sink-tip fly lines, it's important to keep track of the depth at which the fish are located. The best way to do this is to employ a "count-down"

Weedy shallows, such as the area where this canoeing flyfisher has hooked a rainbow, are fished by anchoring the canoe and then using a nymph on a sinking line.

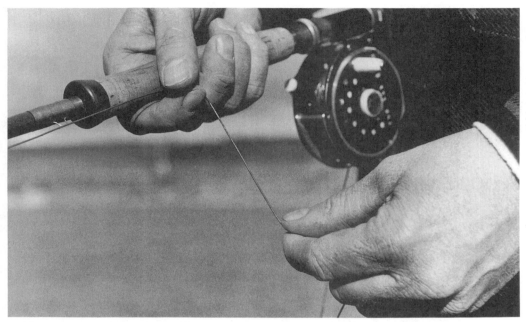

The most commonly used retrieve methods include stripping in lengths of line at various tempos . . .

and hand-twisting the line to cause the fly to crawl along.

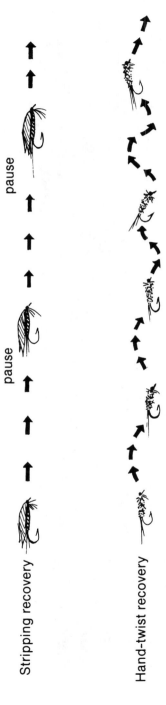

The kinds of action imparted to the fly by the stripping and band-twist recoveries.

while letting the fly sink. My method is to mentally say: "one-one thousand . . . two-one thousand . . . three-one thousand . . . etc." until the fly contacts the bottom or weeds, when the retrieve is begun. Subsequent casts will be made to a depth a count or two less, so that the fly swims along the top of the weed growth, rather than through it. If the area being fished contains freshwater shrimps or snails, then it may be necessary to crawl the fly directly through the weeds or along the bottom.

A devastating technique for attracting trout to a fly being worked over soft lake bottoms lacking extensive weed growth is to let the sinking line carry the fly all the way to the bottom. The fly is then hand-twisted or stripped along so that it kicks-up clouds of debris as a natural might do. This is perhaps one of the deadliest methods of retrieving nymphs over silt or mud bottoms in channels between weed growth.

The tempo and style of retrieve should be gauged to the type of natural food organism being represented. A general rule of thumb to follow is "fast-moving natural, fast-retrieve; slow-moving natural, slow retrieve." But experimentation needs to be freely done to determine the precise retrieve technique most effective at the time. Listed below are the basic retrieves I've found to be most effective in weedy shallows for different types of flies fished on sinking and sink-tip lines.

• Dragonfly nymph: full-sinking line; short, quick strip-ins of line with intermittent pauses.

• Damselfly nymph: sink-tip line during hatching periods, otherwise full-sinking line; slow, regular hand-twist retrieve; in very shallow water, use a floating line and slightly weighted nymph to cause the fly to rise towards the surface during the recovery.

• Mayfly nymph: sink-tip line during hatches, full-sinking line otherwise; slow, irregular hand-twist recovery varied with pauses and short, slow strip-ins.

• Leech fly: full-sinking line with nine- to ten-foot leader and unweighted fly. The objective is to get the leech to undulate slowly like the natural. I use slow, regular strip-ins to do this, few pauses in the retrieve.

• Shrimp fly: full-sinking line; naturals either crawl or "jump" actively amongst the weeds when disturbed. Work the fly in or very close to the weeds using short, quick strip-ins and lots of pauses, or a slower hand-twist with pauses.

• Snail fly: full-sinking line; the best imitation I've found is the O'Gara's Shrimp fly made from natural, gray muskrat fur. Crawl this right along the bottom or through the weeds using a slow hand-twist.

• Streamers suggesting minnows: use a full-sinking line and vary a strip-in recovery to emulate the erratic swimming and darting about of live minnows.

• Caddis pupa: floating lines with weighted flies, or sink-tip lines sometimes produce faster action than full-sinking lines when caddis are pupating to hatch. The objective is to suggest the rising of the pupa towards the surface. Recovery methods may need to vary from slow hand-twist to moderate strip-ins. When pupae are near the surface, and the breeze is blowing briskly, casting across the wind and letting the fly drift freely with occasional strip-ins produces good action. Strikes in this instance may

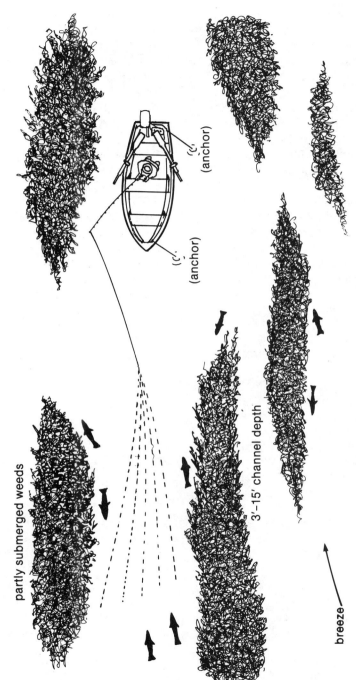

partly submerged weeds

3'–15' channel depth

(anchor)

(anchor)

breeze

Positioning the boat and casting to a weedy lake channel.

not be felt. Look for flashing sides of fish turning to take in the artificial. If caddis are tiny, use a strike indicator on leader and move fly ever so slowly.

Drop-offs

A drop-off is that part of the food-shelf falling away into deeper water in a relatively abrupt fashion. From the standpoint of the fly fisher, the drop-off can be viewed as the *transitional zone* separating the food-shelf from depth-cover. Rainbow trout use it both as a travel-route leading them to abundant food and a zone in which to feed on roving schools of forage fish, which also may feed in the shallows. Because of this, the drop-off can be viewed more as an *intermittent* prime than a consistent one.

In most of the better trout lakes I have fished, the drop-off has been where I have found the largest concentrations of rainbows in the late spring, summer, and early fall days. At times it may offer opportunities for both dry-fly and emerger fishing, as well as for deep nymphing and streamer fly fishing. Unless a hatch is emanating from the deeper end of the food shelf, one can normally look for trout activity from mid-morning to late-afternoon, when the trout move from the shallows to the depths or when they return to the shallows.

Some of the best fly fishing I've had at drop-offs has taken place on certain tea-colored Canadian lakes having Kamloops rainbow trout. In some of these lakes, I have located drop-offs in relatively shallow eight- to ten-foot depths that coincided with the bottom limit of where light penetration allowed weed growth. Mooch-trolling these drop-offs with leech-imitating wet flies has produced

some of the heaviest rainbows I have caught on flyfishing tackle. In one lake, no larger than a mile long by a half-mile wide, I hooked a rainbow that shattered the tip on one of my venerable split-cane fly rods on the strike.

As one does when fishing alone from a row-boat, I had propped my rod-butt against the rear seat of the boat and set my toe against the grip while taking periodic dips on the oars.

The next thing I knew, the rod tip slashed violently towards the water when the fish hit, slamming the rod tip against the motor-board. This happened despite an extremely light drag-setting on my reel. The trout that jumped appeared to be about thirty inches long and nine or ten inches deep. I guessed its weight conservatively between ten and fifteen pounds. The eight-pound-test tippet fractured on the strike. Fortunately, I had another rod in my car. Unfortunately, the car was parked at the far end of the lake. However, I was able to take two nice rainbows of 3 ½ and 5 ¾ pounds later in the day using the same method along the drop-off.

In addition to wind- or mooch-trolling the fly along the edge of the drop-off, several other approaches produce results at times. If the water is shallow enough inside the drop-off, deep wading and casting using a sink-tip line is a good method. But, by and large, that is not the case. The drop-off zone more normally occurs in water too deep to wade. In that case, a float-tube or small boat can be anchored on the shallow side of the drop-off. Then, casts are directed parallel to or perpendicular to the zone and the fly retrieved in a fashion suitable to the artificial being used.

Drop-offs in rocky lakes are often

Casting parallel to the lake's drop-off zone, which can be clearly seen just to the right of the wading angler, tends to be more effective than casting across the zone.

most effectively fished parallel to the drop-off zone. The reason for doing this is that the rocky drop-off may harbor crayfish. The cast offered parallel to the rocky structures of the drop-off remains within view of fish feeding on the cray-fish for a longer retrieve than presenta-tions cutting across the zone.

In some lakes, the trout feed mainly on forage fish. And when they do, the drop-offs in the lake can be good loca-tions to find them herding schools of forage fish. Trolling is very often the best approach in this situation.

Don't expect to catch a lot of rainbow trout fishing drop-offs. But don't be sur-prised if the trout you do hook there are larger and more aggressive than many you'll find working the shallows.

Submerged Brush and Timber

Some of the finest fly fishing opportu-nities I know of for large rainbow trout exist in relatively shallow impound-ments formed by blocking rivers or creeks. Those in which timber and brush existed before the reservoir filled are ideal rainbow trout habitat in regions having cooler year-round climates.

In some of these impoundments, for-age fish existed in the stream before the

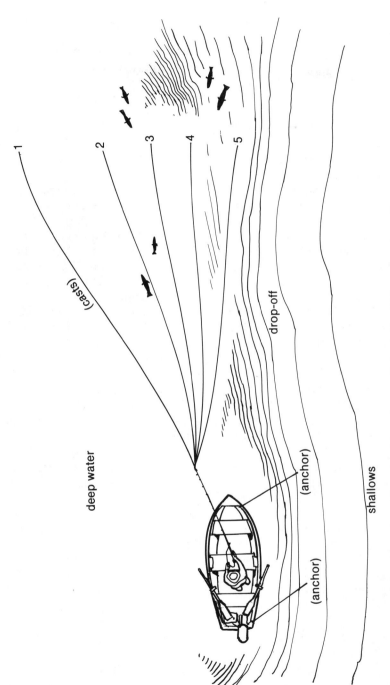

deep water

1

2

3

(casts)

4

drop-off

5

(anchor)

(anchor)

shallows

How to position a boat or float tube for fishing a deep drop-off.

dam was built. In others, aquatic insect life burgeoned in the impoundment after its formation.

One of the best impoundments I have fished was formed by a dam backing up a creek into a finger-shaped meadow a couple of miles long. Most of the timber has crumbled and fallen into the water there, leaving a nightmarish maze of stag-horn-like branches in water.

Rainbow trout already finned in the creek before the dam was built. Later, the fish and game department intro-duced Kamloops-strain rainbows im-ported from Canada.

The first time I fished the reservoir, I stopped to chat with a very old gentle-man who had pulled into shore to eat lunch and doze. His ancient "split bam-boo" three-piece fly rod was rigged with a three-foot-long level leader having two droppers and a terminal loop. To these were tied snelled flies, size 6 White Millers on the droppers and a size 4 Mickey Finn bucktail at the tip-end.

I didn't know a thing about how to go about fishing the lake, so I pulled along-side to see if he could give me any pointers.

"Catch anything?" I asked tentatively.

"I got a couple," he replied with the characteristic reserve of hill-country folk.

I poured myself a cup of coffee, and asked him: "I've got a couple of juicy big Delicious apples in my lunch bag. Wanta share one? I can't eat 'em both."

"Maybe," he said, waiting to see what they looked like.

I took one of the apples out of the bag and bit into it. It was fresh picked and snapped crisply, and squirted juice down my chin when I bit in.

"Sounds good," he grunted. "Maybe I'll try the other one."

We sat there munching the applies si-lently for the better part of ten minutes, him eyeing me suspiciously.

"You catch any?" he finally said, reaching for an ancient canvas kit-bag propped against the back seat of the row boat.

"Only one," I said, "a nice fish of about 15 inches. I released it."

He pulled a peanut butter sandwich out of the bag and began munching on it. As he did that, I happened to glance under the back seat of his boat. The tails of three trout stuck out into the sunlight, each as broad as my hand and fingers were long. The smallest of the three rain-bows appeared to be about four pounds, the largest maybe seven or eight. Next to the rainbows lay a fat-bellied brook trout of perhaps three pounds. To say the very least, the sight of those fish got my juices going!

"How come you released the fish?" he inquired.

"I don't kill any fish, except an occa-sional trout for fryin'," was my reply.

The knowledge I had no intention to take any fish from the impoundment which ran through the old chap's meadow seemed to break the ice. For as he finished his sandwich and poured a cup of coffee, he looked me straight in the eye and said:

"Wanta catch some, like those under the back seat?"

"Yep," I said, as flatly as possible, try-ing to conceal my enthusiasm.

"Why doncha row out there to the edge of the crick channel. You'll see some tree branches stickin' outa the water like an elk's antlers. Tie-off your boat to them."

"Put a Mickey Finn on and cast it where the edge of the channel drops into deeper water. Work the fly slow. The fish're feedin' on young perch. Maybe a little later some caddis'll hatch and you can catch 'em on a White Miller.

"Thanks," I said. "Do you need any more fish, in case I catch a couple of big ones?"

"Nope," said he, "these'll do me till the weekend."

Too old to work cattle any longer, the old fellow obviously was living mainly off the land. We met many times after that. And when we did, there were usually a couple or three huge trout tails protruding from under the back seat of his boat.

I rowed out across the channel and tied-off my boat as he had suggested. My fly boxes hadn't contained any White Miller's since I was a kid. But I had a couple of small Mickey Finns and some large Yellow-and-White bucktails.

Rigging a sink-tip line with a short, stout-tippeted leader, I knotted on a size 4 Yellow-and-White and cast it into the channel, letting the bucktail sink for five long counts. Then I began stripping the fly back in with short, erratic pulls on the line. The rod tip was yanked under the water on the fourth pull. A 20-inch rainbow shot into the air, then raced into the fallen snags and broke off.

Two additional casts with a fresh Yellow-and-White produced smashing hits from 16- to 18-inch rainbows, which I was able to control and bring to release. Then the action stopped cold. I carefully worked two other snaggy areas along the creek channel to no avail.

By this time it was about 2:00 P.M. I stood up to stretch and scan the surrounding waters. There was a swirl near a downed tree in the shallows; then another a few yards off. I untied my boat, rowed over to where I'd seen the swirls and tied off to another snag. A newly

hatched caddis skittered across the water near the snag. Soon, numerous caddis were hatching. I rigged my dry fly outfit with a long, 12-foot leader tapering to 4X. Any fish hooked amongst these snags would have to be played on a tight leash!

To the tippet I knotted a size 10 Carey Special wet fly with a peacock herl body. Another fish swirled in the same manner one usually associates with a trout taking an emerging caddis. I cast a few feet beyond the rise and a bit to one side of the disappearing rings in the water. Then I started slow stripping the fly back. It hadn't moved three feet before it was met with a solid smash from a rainbow in the five-pound class. This fish raced away and jumped over a maze of snags and broke off. I hooked a dozen additional trout from 10 to 20 inches in the ensuing hour. Then the caddis hatch ended and the trout stopped feeding.

In approaching a snaggy impoundment, such as this one, your first inclination is to want to fish it from a float tube or by wading. Both approaches permit keeping a very low profile in the water, which is ideal for sneaking up on trout in the shallows. The problem with wading, however, is that normally the best fishing borders creek channels. Oftentimes, the depth of the water there prevents wading.

Float-tubing extends your reach into the depths, but both the snaggy bottom litter and barbed-wire fences that existed before the pool filled pose hazards. Here again, my personal preference is fishing from a lightweight car-top boat or pram, which draws virtually no water, and because of that, can be easily maneuvered in, out, and over a majority of the snags in flyfishable portions of the impoundment.

Channels in submerged timber and brush often are most effectively fished from a boat, which can be anchored at both ends to permit very straight casts, and which provides a stable platform to fight heavy rainbows.

Outboard motors shouldn't be used in these kinds of water due to the underwater racket they create. The noise of the outboard tends to put the fish off their feeding for some time.

Another reason I opt for the boat is that some such impoundments contain huge trout—fish in the 10- to 15-pound class or larger. Although these larger trout are most often hooked in the open creek or river channel, usually by trolling a two- or three-inch-long streamer fly on a sinking line, the boat provides a higher, more stable platform from which to fight them than the low-profile float tube. A bit more leverage can be put against the fish than can be applied from an anchored float tube. I'm not saying that one shouldn't ever fish such a lake from a float tube. Lack of boat-access sometimes necessitates use of a tube. But it is a heck of a lot easier to fish the channels using the boat, and easier to land any larger fished hooked there.

An outboard motor may be needed to travel the greater distances to ideal fly-fishing grounds on extremely large impoundments. Some are many miles long, encompassing several thousand acres of water.

In these, traveling to and from the fishing grounds may require cautious travel to avoid capsizing the boat or holing its hull on stumps lying just below the surface of the water.

The outboard motor should be turned off several hundred yards from where you intend to start fishing. From that point, the approach should be made using oars or, even better, a quiet-running electric trolling motor.

For the larger reservoirs I fish, my preference for a boat is an aluminum bass boat that draws less than two-inches of water when fully loaded. Mine is rigged with few deck-level fittings that might "grab" loose fly line lying on the deck carpet. Even when fishing from a pram, a piece of all-weather carpeting should be cut to fit the decking. This prevents damage to the surface of the fly line if you accidentally step on it.

There is a tendency of trout inhabiting the tree-choked impoundments to feed in the shallows mainly when forage fish venture there to feed, and when insect hatching is underway. The rest of the time, the larger fish seem to prefer the deeper, cooler creek or river channels. The schools of forage fish tend to cruise up and down the breaklines.

Because of this, trolling frequently is the most reliable way of seeking out the rainbows. This can be accomplished both using sinking fly lines on fly rods, or with lead-core trolling lines fished off conventional revolving spool outfits. When you're fishing alone, and if the impoundment contains rainbows in the ten-pound-plus class, the boat-rod/revolving-spool reel combination, which can be firmly set into a rod holder, has obvious advantages over fly tackle.

When trolling with conventional gear and lead-core line, the best rigging I've found is a 30-foot 6-, 8- or 10-pound-test

monofilament leader nail knotted to the lead-core line.

Since flies as long as six inches may be needed to attract the trout, and because these are relatively heavy in weight, it is rarely necessary to add additional sinker-weight to the long leader. The objective is to get the fly to swim along through the deeper water in as natural a manner as possible. Tandem-hook ties, such as those used for landlocked salmon back East and on the big Deschutes River reservoirs in Oregon, are ideal.

The fly should suggest the prevalent forage fish in the impoundment. Lacking knowledge of that, start fishing with a white one. If that doesn't work, try a yellow one. In the event you can't get strikes on either of those, and a black or grizzly-winged streamer won't produce strikes—don't lose heart, pack up and leave for home after only one day of fishing.

Remember that the big rainbows in the reservoirs and impoundments still tend to pod-up like smaller rainbows. Before locating the fish, you're going to have to locate forage fish. That may take several days on a reservoir spanning 10,000 to 20,000 acres. The fly fishing of the tree-choked impoundment involves far more "hunting" than it does productive fishing. Those lacking patient hunting instincts might best prefer the more predictable lake fishing habitats.

Some of the most interesting and productive submerged timber fly fishing occurs sometimes in natural spring-fed lakes and those formed as parts of flowages. In the former, the flooded timber and brush at the low-lying end may have resulted from a rancher building a low dike to retain runoff waters. This may have resulted in the lake level having

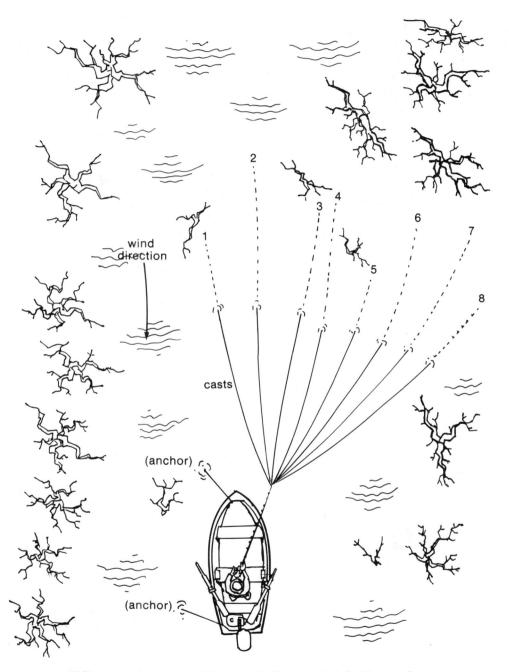

Fishing a wind-current condition in a shallow, stump-choked impoundment.

risen several feet during heavy runoffs. Leeches, dragonflies, and damselflies seem greatly attracted to these shallow, cluttered waters. And it is in them that wind-driven water movement sets the stage for the need of stream-fishing tactics in channels between the brush and timber running in the direction of the prevailing wind.

The *wind-current* conditions most often affect the tactics in water depths ranging from a few inches to four or five feet. A steady wind of fifteen to thirty miles per hour will bring it about. The wind-induced current tends to cause a downwind drifting of free-swimming damselfly and dragonfly nymphs. The

rainbows turn head-into the current, often taking up feeding stations in the channels, just as in a meandering spring creek.

When the trout do this, making casts downwind, because casting may be easier in that direction, produces fewer strikes.

Casts made into the wind or up-and-across it result in the trout being better able to clearly view the fly, as in the broadside drift on a stream.

The trick was disclosed to me by my friend Joe Miotke of Spokane, Washington. One of the better lake flyrodders I have known, Miotke refined this method and developed some deadly lake nymph

Fenton Roskelley with a nice rainbow that tumbled for a nymph fished "upstream" in a wind-current condition on a shallow reservoir. This rainbow was killed for the camp table that night.

flies while fishing North Silver Lake for large rainbows. The most notable of the fly patterns is the Pussycat Nymph. It is designed to suggest a large damselfly or dragonfly nymph and made from a blend of chenille fibers, stripped from the thread core, and cat fur. If you want to know how Joe's cat looked while he developed that fly, ask him. To paraphrase the old saying, there is more than one way to trim a cat!

Submerged Points and Structure

Anyone who has fished for smallmouth bass understands that they are strongly attracted to rocky points of land and underwater rock piles because of the abundance of crayfish and minnows. It's the same with trout. On lakes having rainbows and browns, you will find the fish gravitating to these locations to feed.

Point and structure fishing is done using sink-tip or full-sinking lines because you have to get your fly deep.

Approaches can be made by float tube or by boat. One method involves slowly trolling the deeply sunken fly across the structure, using a wind-drift or occasional dips on the oars. Several passes over the structure are made at increasingly greater depths to assure adequate water coverage with the fly. Another method is to anchor the distance of a long cast from the structure and then fan-cast across the top of it, first from one side, then the other.

When a point holds crayfish, a more effective presentation involves casting from the shore, then retrieving the sunken fly right along the bottom in an "uphill" direction towards the point of land. This provides a far longer retrieve over the point than presentations across the point. It often produces a much larger number of strikes.

When fishing very rocky-bottomed or brushy structures of this sort, one can count on losing a large number of flies to lake-bottom entanglements. That is the price one pays for seeking out large trout in these locations.

A couple of things can be done to minimize fly loss, however. These consist of dressing the flies on keel hooks, in which the hook rides up instead of down, or tying the flies in a weedless style, using a loop of 15- to 20-pound-test monofilament between the butt of the fly and the hook eye in the way of bass flies. I personally prefer the keel hook, because rainbows don't seem to bite down as firmly on the fly as bass. I hook more fish using the keel hook.

Silty Lake Bottoms

Silty lake bottoms provide intermittent bursts of exceptional flyfishing action. Although avoided by many in the mistaken belief that trout rarely feed there, the fact is that in certain lakes much of the trout's underwater feeding takes place over silt or marl. These lakes are dominated by Chironomids and other mud-burrowing species.

The productive lake areas harboring abundant Chironomid larvae may extend to depths in excess of twenty feet. The approach to these may be made both from float tubes and boats. In the deeper areas, casts in excess of eighty feet may be needed to achieve long retrievals near the lake bottom.

What first got me interested in the deep, silty lake bottoms was a discussion I had with Don Earnest, at that time, a distinguished fisheries biologist with the

Washington State Department of Fish & Game. Don was one of the pioneers in lake-rehabilitation and participated in extensive programs to enhance that state's trout fisheries. In the mid-1960s, he was involved in projects to evaluate fishing possibilities on a particular lake located in "scab-rock" country due west of Spokane. His study of the lake, which had extensive silted bottom, indicated that over eighty percent of the trout food there consisted of midge larvae.

A friend and I decided to explore that lake with our fly tackle. We rigged with Hi-D, extra-fast-sinking fly lines and began fishing in fifteen to twenty-five feet of water, using small wet flies and nymphs. Anchoring the boat at both ends to permit very straight underwater retrieves, we would cast eighty or more feet, let the flies sink right to the bottom silt, then slowly hand-twist them back.

Earnest had indicated that most of the midge larvae were of a dark color, about a size 14. Being a fly fisher himself, he thought a small Gray Hackle wet fly or dark-colored fur nymph would probably produce some strikes.

The trout in that lake did not run large, at the time, averaging 10 to 12 inches. But they were numerous. And the long retrieve along the silty bottom did produce some fish.

More recent experiments by others, and the development of a number of very deadly fly patterns to represent the Chironomids, evolved the long-tippet/strike-indicator technique described earlier in the chapter.

Soft lake bottoms also sometimes host burrowing varieties of mayfly nymphs. Some of these include the very large Hexagenia mayflies which drive trout into feeding abandon when they hatch.

Fabulous dry fly fishing often occurs on these lakes over the soft bottoms from which these mayfly nymphs rise to hatch. On eastern and midwestern lakes, where the Hexagenias seem to be more abundant, hatching may occur anytime between May and September, generally over a "marl" lake bottom. (Marl is a crumbly kind of stratum found in streams as well as lakes, consisting mainly of sand, clay, and calcium-carbonate. It is rich in nutrients for the burrowing varieties of mayfly nymphs.) On large, cold western lakes, I've encountered Hexagenia hatches in June and in September, mainly over a silty lake bottom.

Gravel and Rock Shoals

The main attraction of shallow gravel or rock shoals for rainbows is that they resemble the trout's natural spawning habitats in streams. Rainbows in many lakes lacking spawning tributaries tend to congregate on these shoals during the spawning season.

You can identify these shoals by the swirls and wakes of "spawning" trout or by walking the lake shores in search of the gravel formations next to shore.

When the trout are located, the most effective tactic to catch them involves rigging a floating fly line, a long leader, and a wet fly or nymph, having a touch of red in it. A low-profile "sneak" usually is needed to approach the shallows closely enough to make a presentation. You need to be careful doing this on hands and knees in snake country. I've encountered rattlers while doing this at times of year when one would have thought them to be denned-up.

The actual delivery of the fly needs to

The approach needs to be low-profile and cautious when fishing the shallow shoal areas of a lake.

be done so that line and fly land as delicately as possible on the surface. The tactics resemble bone-fishing, in that a fly line casting a shadow across the trout often results in it being spooked and making a dash for deeper water.

Since the trout located on spawning gravel tend to be sexually mature adult fish, large fish tend to be the rule rather than the exception. Some of the best opportunities to fly fish for very large rainbows on huge impoundments are to be had when the fish are on the gravel shoals. Though the fish may be dark in color, the shallow-water battles they offer aren't to be sneezed at. Personally, I don't care to take any fish caught while

spawning. The quality of the flesh when they're in that condition often is inferior to that of fish in prime summer or fall condition.

Inlet Streams

Inlet streams flowing into lakes can be looked upon mainly as intermittent fly-fishing opportunities for rainbow trout. In most that I have fished, the attraction to the trout has been the need to spawn, an opportunity to gorge on spawning forage fish or smolts, or an influx of hatching insects. As indicated earlier, there are inlets which are closely associated with prime feeding areas, such as weedy shallows. And in these instances they tend to attract and hold rainbows in the shallows when rising water temperatures elsewhere might otherwise push them toward deeper, cooler zones of the lake.

The tactical approach to the inlet really is no different than that of fishing a riffle or rapids flowing into a pool on a stream. Dry flies are usually presented up and across the current to minimize drag. Nymphs, wet flies, and streamers are more often presented using a broadside or down-and-across-current delivery. If streamer flies are being used, then stripping retrieves may be desirable as the fly sweeps across the current.

When the trout have pushed well up into the current, a presentation directed from the shore may provide action. At other times, the waters further out into the lake are most effectively fished from a float tube or anchored boat.

The choice of the most suitable fly line for fishing inletting water is dictated both by the type of fly being used and the depth and speed of the current being fished, as in stream fishing.

Special flies are sometimes developed locally to represent spawning forage species. The fly fisher would do well to inquire locally about those patterns, for they vary considerably in size and color. Over the years, I have accumulated a

The inlet stream is fished more effectively from a boat or float tube than from the shore. Stream tactics are used in the presentations to the moving water.

number of dressings, such as Tommy Brayshaw's "Alevin," which I extract from my file and tie when venturing to the particular lake where it's known to be effective.

The rest of the time, I carry a selection of Marabou Muddlers in sizes ranging from 8 through 2, 3XL. These I dress in five colors: white, yellow, gray, olive, and black. They allow me to catch rainbows practically anywhere in the United States and Canada where fishing a minnow-imitator is indicated.

Outlet Streams

Like inlets, streams flowing from lakes afford intermittent flurries of good fly fishing for rainbow trout. Although this fishing may be occasioned by hatches or by the presence of lake-inhabiting forage fishes such as kokanee or ciscoes, the tactical approach to outlet currents is like fishing any other similar sort of stream conditions. What was said earlier about stream tactics is most applicable.

Underwater Rock Cliffs

Of all the lake habitats offering possibilities to catch large rainbow trout, near-vertical rock formations harboring crayfish certainly must rank near the top of the list. Because the crayfish are most active at night, however, the underwater cliffs tend to receive very little fishing

Lake outlets normally offer intermittent flyfishing opportunities. This fly fisher is fishing a dry fly at the onset of a caddis hatch, using a "free-float" in the gentle, slow-moving current.

The author scouts rocky cliff areas like this to determine where he'll be able to effectively mooch-troll crawdad-like wet flies.

pressure, even from the most energetic and avid fly fishers.

To give the reader a better feel for what is involved, let me describe a typical evening's fishing over one. What happened that evening, and later into the night, more or less answers all the tactical questions one might have about the character of the water and the ways to fish it. I won't bother to name the lake, because it is characteristic of innumerable natural and artificial lakes from Washington state east through New England, and from there south into Tennessee. About the only difference between them will be the particular kind of rock from which the underwater cliffs are formed. Most of these will harbor crayfish.

This lake contained two species of trout, both of which feed on crayfish. My targets, however, were the rainbows, which in that lake ran to very respectable size—over six pounds.

It was late June. The rainbows had pretty much vacated the weedy shallows during the day in favor of cooler haunts. The early spring feeding binge of trout on the insect life had ended. I reasoned that a good chance existed for the fish to be feeding actively at night in deeper water on the crayfish. One particular vertical rock shoreline appeared ideal for the search. So I arrived at the lake at sunset. I was prepared with sufficient warm clothing and snacks to stay the night on the lake, if need be, although that turned out to be unnecessary.

Earlier in the week I had carefully scouted the rocky shoreline in bright sunlight from a boat, in order to determine which sort of tactical approach seemed to be the most practical. Since the waters along the cliff ranged from twenty to well over sixty feet, a very slow mooching troll within a foot or so of the rocks seemed the likeliest to keep a fly where trout had a good chance to see it in the moonlight. The trip had been timed to meet the full moon, so that maximum visibility would be possible to play and land any fish that might be hooked. The full moon also afforded the maximum amount of light to penetrate the clear waters to the depth I'd be fishing, roughly fifteen to twenty feet down on a fast-sinking fly line.

Since the crayfish in that lake were a sort of brick-red on the back and cream-colored on the bottom, I had tied a couple of dozen wet flies of similar color and size. I doubted that fly color would be important under moonlight and concentrated more on achieving a suitable silhouette in the ties.

I rigged up a substantial 9-weight fly rod with an appropriate fast-sinking line and affixed a six-foot leader with a 3X tippet. About a foot above the fly I pinched on a small split-shot, so that the line and leader would sink at about the same rate.

Then I motored quietly across the lake to the rocky cliffs, slipped the oars into heavily greased oarlocks, cut the motor and munched a sandwich until I figured it was dark enough for the crawdads to move out from their rocky lairs. The moon came up, bright and creamy. A loon giggled farther down the lake. Mosquitos hatched and bit. Bats from a rock cave across the lake flew out to feed on them and a few late-hatching caddis. The lake's surface was like onyx, smooth and silky in the moonlight. A hush of warm breeze wafted the smell of wood smoke and jack pine my way. I was tempted to simply lie down in the bottom of the boat and let the lapping waters lull me to sleep. But I thought better of it when the reason I had come broke through the reverie.

I pulled on the oars until only a scant oar length from the rocky shoreline. Then I made a long cast ten feet out from the bank, so as not to hook-up on the underwater shelf of rock next to shore. Letting my fly line sink to some thirty "counts," I took a couple of pulls on the oars to straighten the line and to cause the boat to coast closer to shore. I had selected a wooden rowboat for the task, so that it would create less disturbance than my aluminum car-topper when contacting rocks.

Suddenly, my rod tip slashed down and line began to peel steadily from the reel. I grabbed the rod, anticipating a large trout at leader's end. But I'd only hooked a rock. I had to back up the boat in order to retrieve the fly.

This was repeated for nearly an hour. Cast, let the fly sink, take a dip on the oars to start the boat moving, hook a rock, back up and try to extricate it from some unseen, rocky ledge lying deep below the surface. By this time it was about 9:30 P.M. A cool breeze had come up. So I slipped on a jacket and continued fishing.

About 10:00 P.M. I had just tied on my sixth fly and started to drift along the

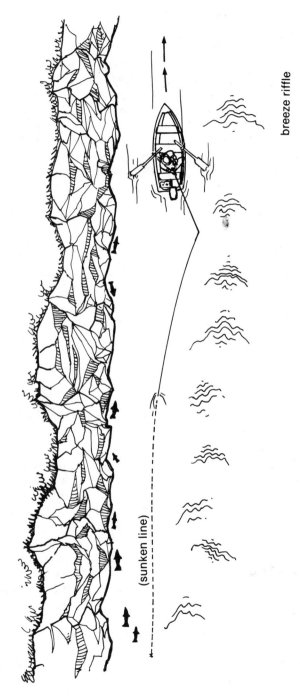

breeze riffle

(sunken line)

How to mooch-troll an underwater rock cliff.

cliff on the breeze. Again, down went the rod tip as earlier. I picked up the rod expecting to feel no more than a solid rock ledge. But this "ledge" was moving . . . moving fast. Then I heard a loud splash in the ebonite blackness of the surface waters further into the lake. I reeled in fast, tightening up against a heavy fish moving rapidly back towards the boat. Ten minutes later I netted a five-pound rainbow, deep-bodied, with a broad, brick-red swath of color down its side.

After releasing the fish, checking the tippet, and making another long cast parallel to the shore, I took a pull on the oars to straighten the line. Immediately, the rod tip slashed down and I was fast to a second trout, which felt a bit smaller than the first. A few minutes later I netted and released a 3½-pounder. Six more trout fell for the tactics by midnight, when the chill in the air and drowsiness prompted me to leave the water.

Since that time, I've repeated these same tactics on similar lakes in other locales. When conditions were right, they have met with success.

Should the reader decide to try them on lakes in his or her region, my best advice is to be prepared to lose a lot of flies for the privilege of hooking a few large trout. To me, it's always worth it.

Wind-riffles

Wind-riffles are the lake-equivalents of food-collecting current-edges on trout streams. Rainbow trout tend to *cruise* the edges of the wind-riffles where they meet slick-surfaced water during Chironomid and mayfly hatches and spinnerfalls, slurping up the hatching or dead insects in deliberate head-and-tail rises.

The tactical approach to fishing the wind-riffles and slicks is to rig a floating fly line with a long, fine leader and dry fly, then cast to the "chain-feeding" fish. Because the trout are constantly on the move—up and down the wind-riffle—it is necessary to watch a certain fish rise a couple of times to be assured of its direction and the intervals between the rises. The cast is then made to "lead" the fish by approximately the same distance as previously occurred between its rises. Sometimes this may be as little as a couple of feet; at other times by as much as ten or fifteen feet.

Although the phenomenon can be considered an intermittent flyfishing opportunity, in the northern regions of the United States it is a predictable one in the fall, and sometimes into early winter, when large-sized Chironomids (size 14 and 12), known as "snow flies," tend to hatch. Some lakes, such as Hebgen Lake in Montana, have become world famous for the fishing to these "gulpers," both brown trout and rainbows.

Others are little known outside their immediate locale, but they afford a similar period of superb dry-fly fishing. When I resided in the Pacific Northwest, two relatively small lakes in the Idaho Panhandle provided outstanding October fly fishing during the Chironomid hatches. And for a twenty-year period, there was scarcely a Saturday morning in October when Tommy Stouffer and I weren't afloat on one of the lakes hoping to meet both the hatch and the right breeze conditions creating the best fly fishing.

Perhaps the most outstanding of these adventures occurred on a morning when the atmospheric conditions were the most unpleasant. We arrived at the lake

When rainbows are chain-feeding on hatching Chironomids, small pods of fish frequently cruise the edges of wind-riffles, where hatched midges accumulate.

about 3:30 A.M., breakfasting at a favored truck-stop restaurant enroute, as was our habit.

The air temperature hovered near 34 degrees F. A thick blanket of ground-fog enveloped the water like a layer of whipped cream on a pumpkin pie. The air was dead-calm. First light would come in an hour or two, but we liked to be on the water when that happened, since some of the best fishing took place at that time. So we unloaded Tom's fourteen-foot car-topper and skidded it into the water.

Then we carefully rigged 6-weight nine-foot fly rods with well-greased floating lines, long, 5X leaders, and tiny midge-like dry flies—a local pattern erroneously tabbed a "Brown Ant."

We also rigged similar floating-line outfits with small nymphs suggestive of Chironomid emergers, in the event the trout were more interested in a fly fished just below the surface.

This accomplished, we sipped final cups of coffee, stepped into the boat, and rowed onto the lake and into the fog bank. We continued rowing until we figured we were well onto the 250-acre expanse of water. An hour passed.

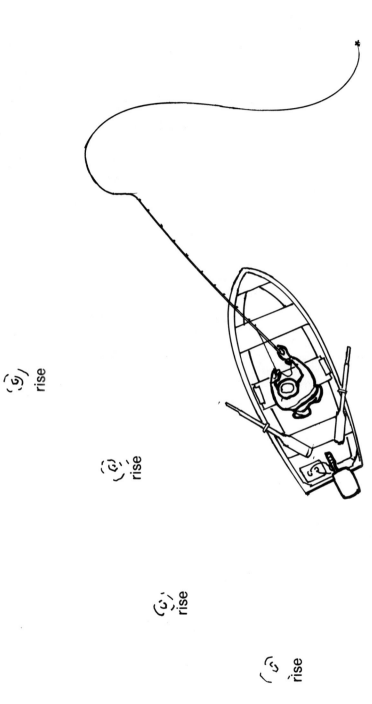

cast here

rise

rise

rise

rise

When flyfishing a Chironomid hatch, the trout normally will chain-feed, rising along the edge of wind-riffle in three to twenty foot intervals. To present the fly to these fish, observe the several rises. Then, make the cast to where you anticipate they will rise next. Once the fly is on the water, DON'T MOVE IT! You are more likely to get a response from the trout if you simply let the trout "find" your fly.

Although we couldn't see the fish, we heard a few sucking early-hatching midges from the water. Visibility was limited to within fifteen feet of the boat. And in this fishing, it had been our experience that casting blind to trout feeding on Chironomids was utterly unproductive.

A little breeze ruffled the water about 5:30 A.M. By six o'clock enough of the fog had cleared to see rising trout. And were they rising! Wherever a wind-riffle met a slick, rainbows could be observed cruising the edge, sucking in the hatching midges with evident relish.

Tom was the first to connect. He had the right "combination" for certain with regard to retrieve: None at all! I had unwisely opted to use a delicate hand-twist retrieve. By 8:00 A.M. Tom had hooked and released nine rainbows between ten and twenty inches in length. I had missed one half-hearted rise, due mainly to my stubborn refusal to fish the fly more slowly.

Although I managed to gain control of retrieve speed during the ensuing hour, I failed to connect with all but a single 12-inch trout. Tom had continued to hook and release nice rainbows, seemingly at will. Although he's not the sort of chap to make you uncomfortable when he's catching 'em and you're not, I kept on trying to coax a strike with feverish determination. I wanted to hook at least one trout that would put a deep bend in the rod!

It finally happened about 9:30 A.M., when the hatch was nearly concluded and the rises had become few and far between.

I had detected a shimmering of the water where the wind-riffle met a slick. A moment later, there was a similar shimmering a few feet further along the seam. "I wonder if that's a rainbow?" I mused, more to myself than to Tom.

Making a cast three feet ahead of the now disappearing "shimmer" I let the fly rest motionless on the water. It sat there for a moment, then disappeared in a satisfied "slup!" I lifted the rod and the reel screeched! This was a very nice rainbow, indeed.

The fish raced away fifty feet, then slashed across the surface low to the water. Then it jumped again, swapped ends and raced for our boat, me stripping in line as fast as possible to keep pace.

The trout jumped again an oar-length away, doing an end-over-end and landing smack dab inside the space between the rear seat and motor-board.

Tom and I both roared our delight!

"That's terrific!" he chuckled, obviously pleased that I had connected with a good fish.

I reached down with a soft towel and grasped the trout, which was still "green" and active. I quickly removed the fly from its lip and slipped it back into the water. It weighed a solid three pounds.

"Some fish, eh?" said Tom, still grinning. "What're you going to tell the fly club members at our Press Club lunch on Tuesday," he smiled.

"Shucks," said I, "I'll simply tell 'em the truth—that the fish were jumping into the boat!"

Tommy roared a hearty laugh, chuckling about it all the way back to the boat-launch. A fitting way to end a great morning of fly fishing, and a fitting way to end a book about fishing for rainbows.

Bibliography

Bates, J. D., Jr. *Fishing*. New York: Outdoor Life Books, 1985.

Brooks, J., *Trout Fishing*. rev. ed. New York: Outdoor Life Books, Harrisburg, PA; Stackpole Books, 1985.

Caucci, A., and Nastasi, B. *Hatches*. Woodside, NY: Comparahatch Ltd., 1975.

Close, T. L., Colvin, S. E., and Bassinger, R. L. *Kamloops, Madison and Donaldson Strains of Rainbow Trout in an Oligotropic Lake*. Minnesota Division of Fish & Wildlife, 1985.

Combs, T. *The Steelhead Trout*. Portland, OR: Northwest Salmon Trout Steelheader Co., 1971.

DeFries, B. *New Horizons for Rainbows*. Ontario Ministry of Natural Resources, 1986.

Fiedler, D. "Skamania." *South Dakota Conservation Digest* 54, (1987).

Ford, R. "Wild Trout." *South Dakota Conservation Digest* 50, (1983).

Franklin, R. F., Decker, L. M., and Overton, C. K. *Seasonal Response of Juvenile Steelheads to Stream Enhancement Structures*. US Forest Service, in cooperation with California Department of Fish & Game.

Fry, D. H., Jr. *Anadromous Fishes of California*. California Department of Fish & Game, 1973, rev. 1979.

Gerlach, R. *Fly Fishing the Lakes*. New York: Winchester Press, 1972.

Gerlach, R. *The Complete Book of Casting*. New York: Winchester Press, 1975.

Glover, R. "Home Improvement for Black Hills Trout." *South Dakota Conservation Digest* 54, (1987).

Gordon, S. W. *How to Fish From Top to Bottom*. Harrisburg, PA: Stackpole Books, 1957.

Hanten, R. L. *Fish Stocking Summary for Missouri River Reservoirs*. South Dakota Department of Game, Fish and Parks, Rept. No. 14–1, 1984.

Hassinger, R. L., Hale, J. G., and Woods, D. E. "Steelhead of the Minnesota North Shore." Minnesota Department of Natural Resources, Division of Fish & Wildlife, no. 11 (1974).

Healey, R. *Factors Influencing Fish Behavior.* Mount Vernon, MO: Lakes Systems Division, (white paper).

Hudy, M. *Natural State Trout.* Arkansas Game & Fish Commission, 1986.

Kelly, J. E. and Throne, G. R. "Evaluation of Trophy Regulated Fish Management of the San Juan River," New Mexico Department of Game & Fish, 30 Jan 1986.

Lilly, B. and Schullery, P. *Bud Lilly's Guide to Western Fly Fishing.* New York: Nick Lyons Books, 1987.

McClane, A. J. *McClane's Standard Fishing Encyclopedia.* New York: Holt, Rinehart and Winston, 1972.

McMullin, S. *Upper Bighorn River Fisheries Management Plan.* Montana Department of Fish, Wildlife & Parks, 1986.

McCrimmon, H. R., and Gots, B. L. *Rainbow Trout in the Great Lakes.* Ontario Sport Fisheries Branch, 1972.

McCombie, A. M., and Berst, A. H. "Look to the Rainbow." *Ontario Fish and Wildlife Review* (1975).

Morita, C. M. *Freshwater Fishing in Hawaii.* Hawaii Division of Aquatic Resources.

Salmon Fishing in Pennsylvania. Pennsylvania Fish Commission.

Seifried, W. E. "Flyrodding for Salmon and Steelheads." *Pennsylvania Angler,* October 1987.

Solomon, L., and Leiser, E. *The Caddis and the Angler.* Harrisburg, PA: Stackpole Books, 1977.

Trout of California. California Department of Fish and Game, 1966.

van Velson, R. C. *The McConaughy Rainbow . . . Life History and Management Plan for the North Platte River Valley.* Nebraska Game and Parks Commission.

Federal Aid in Fish Restoration and Anadromous Fish Studies. Alaska Division of Sport Fishing, 1 July 1985-30 June 1986.

Index

References to illustrations are printed in italics.

Some other fine fishing books
from America's Great Outdoor Publisher

Simplified Fly Fishing
It gets you on the water and fishing with flies in half an hour.
by S. R. Slaymaker II

Handbook of Hatches
A basic guide to identifying trout foods and selecting flies to match them.
by Dave Hughes

Reading the Water
A fly fisher's handbook for finding trout in all types of water.
by Dave Hughes

Joe Humphreys's Trout Tactics
by Joe Humphreys

Learn How to Fly Fish in One Day
Quickest way to start tying flies, casting flies, and catching fish.
by Sylvester Nemes

Nymphing
A basic book.
by Gary A. Borger

Naturals
A guide to food organisms of the trout.
by Gary A. Borger

Tying and Fishing the Fuzzy Nymphs
Fourth edition, revised, updated, and enlarged.
by E. H. "Polly" Rosborough

Fishing the Midge
by Ed Koch

Basic Freshwater Fishing
Step-by-step guide to tackle and know-how that catch the favorite fish in your area.
by Cliff Hauptman

Available at your local bookstore, or for complete ordering information, write:
Stackpole Books
Cameron and Kelker Streets
Harrisburg, PA 17105
For fast service, credit card users may call 1-800-READ-NOW.
In Pennsylvania, call 717-234-5041.